I0820527

The Secret Mind

The Secret Mind

UNLOCK THE POWER OF DREAMS TO TRANSFORM YOUR LIFE

Bonnie Buckner, PhD

Urano
publishing

Argentina - Chile - Colombia - Spain
USA - Mexico - Peru - Uruguay

© 2025, by Urano Publishing, an imprint of Urano World USA, Inc

8871 SW 129th Terrace, Miami, FL 33176 USA

Urano
publishing

Cover design by Amanda Weiss

Cover illustration copyright © berkahlineart / Adobe Stock

Illustrations on pages 163, 166, 170, 176, and 183 by Katalin Pula

Cover copyright © Urano Publishing, an imprint of Urano World USA, Inc.

The first edition of this book was published in July 2025.

ISBN: 9781953027467

E-ISBN: 1953027466X

Printed in Colombia

Library of Cataloging-in-Publication Data

Buckner, Bonnie PhD

1. Personal Growth 2. Business

Dedication

To my father and grandmother, my first teachers of dreaming.
And to dreamers everywhere.

Table of Contents

NOTE: In most instances, dreamers' names have been changed.

Introduction

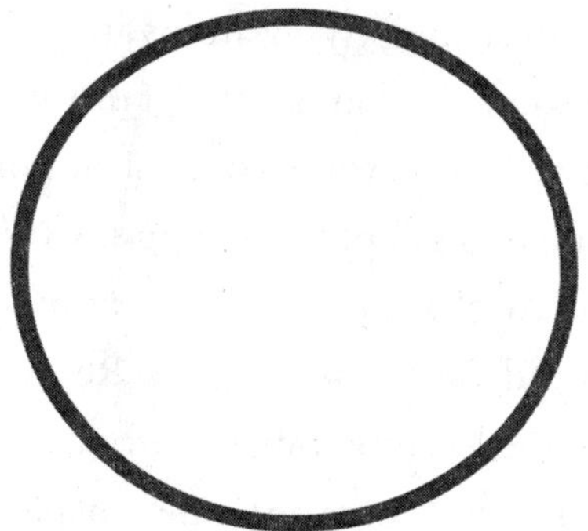

What do you see?

If you are eight or nine years old reading this you will see many things—the top of a fence pole, a porthole on a ship, or maybe a monster's eyeball. The image above is an example of one kind of question found on tests for measuring creativity.[1] When this test is given to elementary schoolkids, there are about ninety unique answers per group. They envision it as a cave that a tiger is about to leap out of, or the rim of a bike wheel ridden by a superhero; it might be a manhole cover in a street or the entrance to a tunnel through a mountain. When junior and senior high school kids take the test, though, those ninety unique answers per group drop to about twenty or fewer. When this test is given to adults, it's a big goose egg, except that they don't see that; adults get only an average of two answers per group, including the obvious: "it's a circle" or "it's a circle on a white page".[2]

From an exciting tiger's cave to a boring circle. Why?

Creativity underpins every aspect of the human experience.[3] Life is a project, and we use our creative faculties to inventively figure out how to pay our bills, raise children, advance our careers, and fundraise for organizations. We design alternative costumes for our child's school play when the first one is ruined and conceive new slides for a presentation when a meeting abruptly changes. It's such a part of our everyday problem-solving that we often overlook it. Employers don't, though; useful as creativity is in our everyday, it is also the treasured aspect underlying innovation.

The World Economic Forum's 2023 Future of Jobs Report lists creative thinking as one of its top two most important skills, citing it as critical to the ability to adapt to changing workplaces.[4] In the last ten years IBM[5] and Adobe[6] listed it as a number one searched-for quality in hires. So did Bloomberg's Jobs Report—except that they also included this note: recruiters want it, but they aren't finding it.[7]

Since 1990, creativity scores in America have been sharply declining among both adults and children.[8] Despite the necessity of creativity in our daily and professional lives, America is undergoing a "creativity crisis."

Creativity has been tracked worldwide in both children and adults since 1966 via the Torrance Tests of Creative Thinking ® (TTCT). In general, creativity fluctuates as we develop. Around the age of eight or nine, for example, there is the "fourth grade slump." Both creativity and curiosity decline before increasing again around sixth grade. This is around the time socialization and conformity are first taught, and many studies have suggested this as the dampening agent behind the slump. The creative skill of elaboration also declines with age. Elaboration is the ability to think in a detailed and reflective manner, as well as the *motivation* to be creative. To continue to work with an idea, to think deeply about it and develop its myriad possibilities, one must be motivated to do so. Not everyone loses this skill, though. Some individuals continue to develop it, a key point which we will come back to in a later chapter. And as you may have guessed, fluency, which is the ability to produce ideas, also declines—that's why kids see a round shape ninety different ways while adults see only a circle.

Despite these general fluctuations, since 1990, creative thinking across *all* age groups, and *all* categories of measurement, has been progressively on a downward slide. Researchers are finding that people are steadily losing even the creative skills that normally increase with age: the ability to find the essence of a problem and think critically, for example. Most concerning of all, though, is that this decline is starting as early as kindergarten, meaning even skills that usually build throughout the developmental process are stunted.

How many things can you imagine a circle to be? A circle that provokes nearly endless possibilities, or a circle that is seen as just a circle—the implications of the loss of possibility are dire. Creativity researcher Mark Runco asks college students to list everything that might impede their graduating and then to choose one of those items and come up with as many solutions for it as possible. Some of these students can list numerous things that might go wrong but are then unable to find any solutions. Not being able to see beyond a problem—to imagine something different—is despairing. In fact, the inability to conceive of solutions is predictive of suicidal ideation even when controlling for preexisting levels of depression and anxiety.[9]

It may seem strange to begin a book about dreaming by talking about creativity. But creativity and dreaming are intimately linked. They use the same neurological processing system, called the **default network.**[10] This system of cognition is not only responsible for imagination, but also emotional regulation, social perspectives and empathy, and meaning-making. This network, and the larger social brain, is intensely active in dreaming, processing memories, and regulating emotions.[11] Creativity is an essential component of empathy, where in order to feel for the other, we have to imagine stepping into their shoes and view new forms of interaction and relationship.[12] Not surprisingly, then, children who score lower on creativity tests exhibit higher aggression than children who are assessed as more creative.[13]

Creativity research has found that today's young people are growing up "more narrow-minded, less intellectually curious, and less open to new experiences."[14] A sobering list of things young people are losing includes imagination, perception, the ability to synthesize information, and the motivation to look at things from different perspectives.[15] Imagination, creativity, and play, once the established domains of children, are now on the endangered list. Yet these very aspects that adults mistakenly tried to "mature" kids out of are turning out to be the skills all of us—adults and children—need the most.

Narrow-minded kids grow up to become narrow-minded adults. Of the many dire problems we collectively face in the world today, one is a trend toward political extremism. That narrowed perspective, as well as the shrinking motivation to seek new perspectives, also has consequences for other problems we are facing, such as climate change. Young people's sense of climate change these days is characterized by hopelessness, and rather than this outlook inspiring action, it is associated with a *lack* of environmental engagement.[16] One can't help but think of Runco's students who found numerous problems but were unable to suggest any possible solutions.

The default network is a vital piece of our cognition. And yet, much to the alarm of neuroscientists, there are numerous factors getting in the way of our spending time nurturing and utilizing it. It gets utilized in sleep through dreams, and in waking time when we stop focusing and allow our minds to wander, imagine, and float freely, but these windows of opportunity are closing. Technology is one factor that pulls us away from daytime unfocused reflection. Our phones also disrupt deep sleep.[17] Add to that the shift in schools to standardized testing, the data-obsessed and overly serious nature of business, overscheduling, lack of play, and biases that favor known efficiency over the uncertainties of the creative process and trying out new ideas[18] and the default network, with its critical cognitive processes, is pushed to the periphery.

All told, our society is forgetting to dream. It may be the most critical problem facing society today.

Dreaming lifts our minds beyond the constraints of the everyday. Creativity turns these ideas into things and brings our greatest imaginings into waking realities. It is by using the engine of our creative imagination that we work through the "how" of manifesting our life's dreams; entertaining possibilities, elaborating upon them, and imagining alternative scenarios. It is our innate source for problem-solving. Life really is the stuff of imagination; if we are able to see it, we can find a way to make it. In a direct ratio, the limit of our imagination is the limit of our living.

This is a book about dreaming. It is also a book about creativity. Some neuroscientists call dreaming a hypercreative state,[19] and one of the arguments that will be made in this book is that the two are synonymous in origin. We access our creativity through dreams and our spontaneous imagination, simultaneously reaching our innate problem-solving capacity and developing that system of cognition the same way we would develop a muscle through a workout.

Creativity can be developed[20] and the creative slumps we go through can be circumvented. My approach to working with dreams develops creative skills, offering an antidote to the creativity crisis. I will teach you, for example, how night dreams show us where we are blocked in waking life, how to identify these blocks, and unlike Runco's students, unlock your fluency skills to come up with numerous ways to overcome them. You will develop the critical skills needed to choose which of these possible solutions is the best fit and learn how to work with multiple perspectives to imagine numerous outcomes. You will learn that some of our night dreams reveal hidden personal potentials, and how night dreaming and waking dreaming can be bridged, so that you can bring your conscious attention to subconscious mechanisms to fuel real change in your life. More than anything, you will learn how to dream beyond self-imposed limitations and bring those dreams into waking manifestation.

It is each of us, collectively, who are the creators of families, organizations, governments, and societies. If we lose our ability to dream—to imagine a world we want to live in and the means by which we can create it—where is our future? The study I've been referencing has been tracking the declining creativity scores for over two decades; many of those first children studied are already moving into adulthood. Their, and our, future is now.

The Great Dream of Self

Dreaming as a society begins with the individual dreamer. Our first and greatest lifelong creative project is our own. Our first task of the imagination, then, is to envision who we are and the life we want to live. At its core, this is a book to help you do that.

Within each of us is a Great Dream of Self. It is the "who" we know we are capable of becoming, and the "what" we are interested in discovering in order to one day contribute our own uniqueness back to the world.

Our mission in life, if you will, is to discover this Great Dream of Self, and engage with it to bring to fruition all our potentials, to develop this uniqueness to its fullest possible expression. When we do, we fill in a missing piece in the grand puzzle of humanity, illuminating a perspective that only each of us holds. By realizing our fullest individual potential, we bring fresh ideas and adaptive traits that make collective evolution possible.

Simple as it sounds, numerous things get in the way of realizing our Great Dream. At some point during childhood, an adult, parent, or teacher tells us that one of our ideas is silly, or the subject of our passion is ridiculed, or we are told that what we most want to do in the world is impossible. In these moments we separate from our Great Dream, putting more and more distance between us and our true self, hiding our talents and desires. Remember the fourth-grade creative slump that occurs at the time social conformity is taught? Pleasing family and seeking to fit in are the first gaps we put between ourselves and our dreaming.

Returning to this dreaming self as an adult and excavating the Great Dream means climbing over the cemented belief systems we set up to justify why we seek to please others instead of following the inner self. Belief systems prioritize external values over our internal ones, causing us to chase goals that satisfy our beliefs but keep us lacking inside. Belief systems work, and are hard to root out, because they *make sense*. If there wasn't some sensible aspect to them, we wouldn't adopt them. It is for this reason that dreaming is our most powerful tool for reconnecting with our inner truth. Dreaming operates outside belief systems, catching us unaware when the patterned, judging aspects of our neurological processing are literally taken offline.[21] Slipping in under the radar in this way, dreams are emotional, physical events that utilize the material of past experience and memory, causing us to remember who we are and return to a felt sense of inner truth.

When we take up this challenge to dream again, life expands. Dreams revive the parts of self we discarded, blamed, or overlooked because they might not be accepted. The powerful, courageous, and persevering aspects of ourselves—the ones we sent to the background because they might cause waves—are freed to step to the forefront. We access an inner, peaceful joy, even as we move through life's inevitable ups and downs, because our inner conflict of not living our true self resolves.

When we don't take up the challenge, however, we diminish who we are, robbing both ourselves and the world of what we can and want to contribute. Because of that, disappointment and cynicism set in, closing the heart and causing us to be negative and distrustful of the goodness of what the self, life, and others have to offer. These emotional tangles in our inner world get projected out onto others, creating conflicts in all areas of our lives. We blame others and circumstance when, in fact, it is our own self-stifling that is responsible. In this restricted state we tend to let others define us, conforming ourselves to others' paths. Hiding aspects of ourselves makes us feel powerless, and we risk trying to resurrect these hidden parts by hitchhiking on the views of someone else we see as powerful, replicating rather than adding an original piece to humanity's puzzle.

The journey to discover the Great Dream of Self includes reconnecting with the truth of our being and envisioning a whole new way of living, as well as overcoming the nightmarish blocks that get in the way of doing so. None of this can be done through thinking; rather, it is done through engaging the transformative power of our inner, creative imagination—through dreaming. By reconnecting with the dream of self, we literally dream our Self into being.

The Secret Mind

For over two decades, I've been helping people meet their true selves and manifest their inner potentials using an ancient approach to dreaming. Dreaming is the present-tense language of our experiencing, which is always active and responsive. The work I will teach you to do in this book is to speak this present-tense language of the Self so that you can interact directly with the blocks and potentials presented in your dreams to shift your waking present. This book rests on four fundamental points:

1. Dreaming is an ongoing process that occurs both in sleep and in wakefulness, and it is a process that we can become conscious to in either state.
2. Dreams orient us to where we are physically, emotionally, mentally, and spiritually in our present tense and operate as the meeting point of our inner and outer experiencing.
3. Dreams are the means for transformation, both in our personal lives, and as you will see in the last chapter, for entire communities.
4. The material of dreams is meaningful, can be understood, and is meant to be actively engaged with and worked with in order to unlock transformative potential. Dreams are a practical tool for creativity and change.

The Secret Mind is so called because even though dreaming is active at all times, it lies hidden in plain sight. Our waking life is crowded with activities that focus our attention on specific tasks or goals. In the background of our inner world, however, we have inner responses to all the experiences happening to us—both the ones we are focusing on, and the ones we aren't. We find these responses in the images of our night dreams and in our waking spontaneous imagination.

Put simply, dreaming and imagery tie together the whole of our experience: what we are consciously focused on and that which we aren't; our outer doing, and our inner reflecting. It organizes our experiences into coherent images for us to literally see and understand the full picture of our present—how we feel about it, understand it, and how we are reacting to it in our inner sphere. Because dreams have access to all parts of us, they also show other possible responses and perspectives that are available. It connects the memories of our past to the new information being received, and the responses and ideas this elicits become the grist of what determines our future. Dreams, therefore, become the space for meaning-making and potential change for our lives.

By learning how to intentionally access this system of cognition, we access this Secret Mind, connecting our consciousness and vast inner knowing so we can intentionally inform our choice-making. We take what we think of as "subconscious" and bring attention to it, becoming aware of the beliefs and patterns that trigger habitual reactions *before* they engage so that we can change our course. This makes us responsive to life instead of reactive to it.

The Dreaming Background

My own experience with dreaming began with waking from a nightmare at three years old. Because I'd had a series of nightmares, night after night, I wondered if it was possible to never sleep again, to stay awake forever. I even thought briefly of not living anymore at all, so intense were the nightmares and the fear they left me in upon waking. This thought was brought short by thinking that, for all I knew, life after death might be just another long dream. And so, I came to realize that I had one recourse: to understand and master these dreams, to overcome my nightmares. In this moment I had a deep sense that this would be my life journey, and that I would become a teacher of dreams to help others do the same.

From this childhood realization I was carried forward through the hands of the dreamers in my family, my first teachers. Then, years later as an adult, I had a dream in which my then-deceased father literally handed me off to Colette Aboulker-Muscat, the modern teacher of the dreaming and imagery lineage I teach today. Two years later, through another series of dreams, I finally encountered that lineage in waking life when I met Colette's student and longtime collaborator Dr. Catherine Shainberg, with whom I would study for over a decade.

The approach to dreaming taught in this book comes from the thirteenth century, from two Mediterranean rabbis with mystery schools in France and Spain. Their teachings were passed along their family of teachers to the late Colette. Called the Kabbalah of Light, its roots of inner-insight can be found even earlier, dating well before the first century. Colette further developed this work for a modern audience through understandings derived from her studies in philosophy and psychology, and an apprenticeship with her father, the renowned professor of neuroscience, Dr. Henri Samuel Aboulker.

My own academic work has centered around the study of images and their use as cognitive tools for behavioral change and the means through which we build communities, societies, and culture. This research has been multidisciplinary, spanning cognitive psychology, neurobiology, somatic studies, cognitive linguistics, phenomenology, and perceptual geography, among others. Exciting new discoveries in these fields give useful insights and vocabulary to the dreaming lineage, and throughout this book I'll reference them.

There are some important distinctions between the approach in this book and current approaches to dream research. The first lies in the extent of research underlying them. Modern science—and neurobiology and dream research in particular—is quite young. Neurobiology especially relies on technological tools to view the brain at work, and with each more powerful generation of tools, new and often conflicting observations are unearthed. So, while modern science has a tremendous amount to add, as dream researcher Kelly Bulkeley and neuroscientist Patrick McNamara note, we have to be careful to recognize these limitations.[22]

By contrast, the dreaming work of this book has over a thousand years of direct observation and replication that has shown consistent results. We may call it ancient wisdom but it, too, is science. Malidoma Patrice Somé, of the Dagara Culture of Burkina Faso, West Africa, said of some of his grandfather's waking dream practices that he was an "indigenous technologist."[23] I love this phrase and will borrow from Somé that idea to call the ancient dreaming lineage an ancient science that uses ancient technologies.

The second distinction lies in the difference between the perspectives underlying the differing approaches. Most of today's approaches to dreaming have grown out of the field of psychology and neuroscience, which has tended to isolate brain function from somatic experience and is therefore mental in its approach to understanding dreams. The lineage of this book understands the human as a body-mind whole and is particular in its understanding of embodiment and treatment of images as a specific language of the body.

The understandings of this work arose in cultures that were, inherently, deeply embodied and in direct and close relationship to nature. Living under stars and sun, according to the rhythm of the seasons, these early dream scientists were deeply in touch with the senses, physical feedback, and inner communications of their bodies. This is vastly different from how we live now, rushing through fast-paced lives, "in our heads," and separated from nature in man-made cars, offices, and houses.

The minds and perspectives of people and cultures that are in deep relationship to nature—and where the body is central—are entirely different. Their understandings grow out of, and speak to, actual lived experiences, as opposed to academic theory. Modern neuroscience, itself recognizing its own gaps, is increasingly turning to anthropology and the study of indigenous groups as a window to a more embodied, traditional understanding of dreams.[24] It is perhaps this very aspect that makes the lineage of dreaming found in this book such an urgently needed call to healing for our current state of estrangement from Self, Body, Nature, and Source. Returning to dream will return you to your own body and to a sense-based relationship with the world in which you are living.

Embodiment changes everything. It is active and responsive; instead of *thinking about*, like theories do, embodiment *acts on*. The method provided in this book is based on transformation and is meant to be directly applied to your life. While most popular approaches to dreaming focus on the meaning of dreams as a thought exercise, this approach is a way of actively engaging with meaning-making in real time as personal meaning arises from bodily responses to challenge and experience. Instead of merely something to ponder, dreams offer specific means to effect change and growth.

Embodiment also means this work is grounded in reality. Our bodies are calibrated to balance, known as homeostasis. When cold, we shiver; when hot, we sweat. Intrinsically, our bodies understand what is real and what is fantasy, when we're stuck and when we aren't. The mechanism of dreaming, springing from the body, is an internal tool oriented toward maintaining balance.

A final point on the embodied aspect of dreaming is that it makes this work both easy and universally accessible. All of us contain body intelligence, and dreaming is our innate ability to understand ourselves, make change, and create something new. You are your own expert. You have all the tools you need, already—*in you*—to make the changes you want to make in your life. I will show you examples from clients' and my own dreams and how to incorporate these techniques into your own life so that you can understand and work with your own dreams.

This book is written as a scaffolding, moving from beginning considerations of dreaming, to examining specific components of dreams, to putting the components together and working with dreams and their messages, to the final chapters where larger considerations beyond the individual experience of dreaming are discussed. Each chapter contains exercises for:

1. Developing your own dream practice and the ability to be an awake dreamer.
2. Using dreams as tools for transformation.

Chapter One invites you to engage with your dreams as messages from the Self. You will learn how to receive the messages of your dreams, including increasing dream recall. Chapter Two takes you into the embodied, image-based language of dreams. You will learn how each of us builds a unique "image vocabulary" from our experiences, and how these inform dreaming. Chapter Three introduces you to the seven kinds of dreams. You will learn how categorizing dreams can be applied to waking life as you develop the awake dreamer.

Chapter Four looks at how the seven different kinds of dreams fall into two categories—unresolved and resolved—and how to use these categories to bring about resolution to areas of imbalance in your life. Chapter Five looks at the four levels contained within each dream. You will learn how to move through these levels and, as in Chapters Three and Four, you'll learn how to apply these levels to waking life to further develop the awake dreamer. Chapter Six tackles how we can avoid tricking ourselves out of understanding our dreams by looking at two very specific components of dreams that I call the Locating Aspect of images in dreams and the Presenting "I."

Chapter Seven expounds upon a tool for transforming blocks in dreams, including a waking dream exercise. And Chapter Eight lays out a way of directly interfacing with dreaming in waking life. The seven kinds of dreams are overlaid onto a rubric based on the body's energy flow and its expression through instincts, emotions, and feelings. You will learn how to map your own body, direct your body's energy flow to your desired destination, recognize when your dreams are showing you imbalances in this energy flow, and apply tools for shifting it.

Chapter Nine shifts gears a bit, moving from dissecting dream components to looking at the broader dreaming journey. Here we'll start by looking at intuition, how to recognize it, and how to verify it. Chapter Ten turns to what we call Great Dreams and how to use dreams to move through a large life transition. In it we will follow the dreaming journey initiated by a Great Dream of mine, as well as hear other examples from the dreams of my clients. Chapter Eleven builds on this to discuss the powerful influence everyone has for affecting systems and impacting the world through their own dreaming.

The Mystery of Dreaming

Writing a book about dreaming is tricky, because dreaming is present tense, fluid, and contains multiple layers of meaning. In a book, this dynamic aspect of dreaming must be cut into chapters and pages. Dreaming, however, is a vibrant language. At its base are perceptions, experience, and inner knowing, all contained in image and feeling. These understandings shift and deepen as we engage with them, lending even further insights as we walk them through our waking day. Modern minds tend to want to pin down dreams, making fixed interpretations. Dreams, however, *unfold*. The more playful we are with dreaming, interacting with them as a child would, the better.

Dreams are meant to be mysterious; they provoke questions more than answers. Modern science has trained us to think that fact-based knowledge—answers—are the ultimate pursuit. But a shift in school curricula toward more science- and technology-based learning is another of the reasons for what is driving the current creativity crisis.[25] Unlike modern science, the ancient science of dreaming knows that mystery—*wondering about*, not just *knowing that*—is key, not just for creativity, but for all discovery and change.

The questions and curiosity, the bizarre and not-immediately understood aspects elicited by dreams are part of their transformational power. For all that we know, there is so much more that we don't. While modern minds want to dispel mystery or use these mysterious aspects to dismiss the power of dreams, it is that very element that makes them so powerful. What we don't know yet, but curiously explore, is the base of innovation.

A young university student, struggling in class, dreams of a space where all the knowledge he needs is easily accessible. That student was Larry Page, and he built that knowledge space in his dream into Google.[26] The list of society-shifting ideas that come from dreams is vast. From Einstein's theory of relativity to the *Twilight* series.[27] it is the unknown in dreams, the mysterious, that wakes up our imagination, and transforms us as individuals and society. **Mystery is not impediment, but a key to evolution.**

To learn the tool of dreaming, we have to dream. Each of the practices that are suggested in this book are developed with the hope and expectation that the reader will engage with them. They are simple yet powerful. The experience of doing these practices will deepen your understanding of Self and make clear certain points that might otherwise seem opaque. It is only by fully living this work that it becomes integrated and understood.

We all once spoke the dreaming language as children, and it can be relearned. Remember—you are already a dreamer. When working with dreams, the dreamer in you, having woken, will intuit and inform. Simply look inside and listen.

And now . . . what is your dream?

CHAPTER ONE

The Letter

"A dream that has not been interpreted is like a letter that has not been read."
—RAV CHISDA, second-century rabbi[1]

A woman dreams she is standing alongside the River Seine, in Paris, and sees a horse-drawn carriage coming down the bank toward her. Then, she sees a modern motorboat in the water going up the river, away from her. From this she wakes up knowing she can't wait any longer to fulfill her lifelong dream of writing and working in the arts. She quits her job that very day and soon finds employment at a major national publication as a journalist covering the arts, where she has worked ever since.

Which is the dream? That of writing and art? Or the night vision of an old way of moving from an outdated age, seen in the horse and carriage, contrasted with the new mode of this modern time zipping away in the flow to someplace yet unknown? They are one and the same. The old job that no longer fits with the modern self of today, the motor of the true passion that emerges in the waters of dreaming and zips forward, beckoning the dreamer to follow it. Even the speed at which the change was possible—all of it is one dream. Whatever we are living, we are dreaming;

whatever we are dreaming, we are living. Waking life and dreaming life are one.

The Letters of Our Dreams

We are dreaming all the time.

Inside us lie the inner imaginings of ourselves, the world as we understand it, our directions and intentions, and the passions that we yearn to explore and fulfill. This inner self is continually speaking to us, offering instruction, pointing out little-used talents relegated to our peripheries, signaling stagnation, and reminding us of the real enquiries we seek to pursue in our life journey. The question is: *Are we listening?*

Like the epigraph at the beginning of this chapter, dreams are letters from the Self, containing important glimpses into our inner experience; disregarded or unnoticed, however, they are a letter unopened, a message not received. This chapter focuses on how to receive these letters.

There are many reasons people list for not opening the letters of their dreams: they don't dream, they don't have time, they don't consider dreams important, they fear what they say, or they don't understand them. Each of these reasons has little to do with dreaming. Rather they speak to the symptoms of a deeper malaise: not creating time for self-reflection in one's life, judgment and dismissal of the products of our own self-reflection, or fear of facing the Self or current problems. Right from the beginning, then, engaging with dreams begins to address these issues, creating openings to reach beneath symptoms to the deeper problem and begin the healing process. Before even progressing to working with dreams themselves, learning to receive dreams is itself a transformative process.

The most common rebuttal to dreaming that I hear is "I don't dream." It's more accurate to say that one doesn't recall one's dreams. Dreaming occurs during all stages of sleep, REM and non-REM.[2] In studies where participants are awakened during REM sleep, recall is consistently 80 to 90 percent; recall on waking from non-REM stage 2 is about 70 percent. Dream recall has even been recorded when waking from non-REM stage 3.[3]

An interesting study looking at the percentage of individuals who claim to never recall a dream was conducted by sleep expert James Pagel. From a sample of 598 individuals completing a dream survey, 7 percent reported never having a dream or nightmare. Pagel followed up with this small subset and found many actually *did* remember dreams. They either misspoke on the survey, remembered a few dreams from childhood, or started dreaming after their time at the laboratory (a point we'll return to shortly). This dropped the sample to less than 1 percent of people who truly claimed not to recall their dreams.[4] French neuroscientist Michel Jouvet, who has spent his entire career focusing on dreams and sleep, puts it this way: For those who think they don't dream, they "can be reassured, for they do in fact dream every night, but the moment they wake up they wipe out the memory of their oneiric activity."[5]

If we conclude, then, that most if not all people dream, then we have to look at what gets in the way of dream recall. What causes us to wipe out this memory upon waking? This question has multiple answers and the best place to start is around the subject of time, which includes sleep.

It may seem obvious, but if we want to have a night dream, we have to sleep. The science of sleep is clear that today most people don't get enough sleep.[6] We claim the overload of daily life—long work hours, restricted time to spend with family, too many items on the to-do list—is the impeding force that keeps us from sleeping enough. To make this claim, however, is to overlook perhaps the most critical factor that gets in the way of our ability to sleep and to dream: technology.[7]

Technology and Dreaming

It is typical today to load up free time and evenings with news, movies, and interactions with phones and media. The habitual touch of our devices is so familiar that we tend to not think of interacting with them as being tethered to technology. Many households have multiple devices in multiple rooms, including the bedroom. At any given time, some form of technology is either activated or ready to be so. Many devices have sounds, lights, and movements to notify us of activity. Such notifications ensure that the habitual touch is further engrained as the brain locks into anticipating and responding to them. It's not unlike a baby crying.

In the introduction, I mentioned a neurological system of cognition called the **default network.**[8] This important system is responsible for internally focused processing, including that of imagining future and possible scenarios—"trying on" this job or that, rolling around ideas about something we are working on, and so on. It is also the neurological center for social cognition, or experiencing feelings and emotions around social situations. This includes imagining the feelings and perspectives of others—thinking about, for example, how another person felt about a situation or our actions, whether or not it hurt their feelings, or if we crossed a boundary. It handles the recall of personal memories and emotions and is a key figure in the meaning we make of events and situations. The default network is linked to larger creative processes, which we will dive into further at the end of this book.[9]

The default network is also, as you may have guessed, linked with dreaming. Recent studies show that it is at the base of dreaming processes while asleep.[10] The default network starts "thinking" when we stop doing so. In waking time, it kicks into gear when we gaze out the window, let our minds wander, imagine, and daydream (in neuroscience circles, it is variously called each of these things, depending on which study you read). What we think of as just watching clouds drift by—reflective, unstructured, and undirected thinking—is in fact a highly active neurological process critical to our cognition. Too bad we didn't have this information in elementary school when our teacher was telling us to "get our head out of the clouds" and pay attention.

What was that teacher wanting us to do, anyway? That teacher was asking us to focus on externally directed, concrete, and goal-driven tasks that make use of other neurological processing systems, grouped into the **executive network**. This part of the brain's cognitive processing loves, for example, to dive into adding up numbers or data or simply visually focusing on the blackboard. It activates to make decisions—like this place for lunch or that metro line to get home—and to pay attention to external stimuli like a ball being thrown to us, or a phone dinging. The executive network loves attending to all the notifications and tasks that come with technology.

Both the default and the executive networks are necessary aspects of our acting in, and making sense of, our world. In the most simplified of characterizations, we can call the active, outer-focused part of our brain's processing the domain of the executive network, and the inner-focused, reflective, making-sense-of part as belonging to the default network.

The executive network handles the stimuli of everyday life, while the default network reflects on it, incorporates how others have felt about our actions, makes meaning of it, and imagines beyond it. The oscillation between active, goal-driven processes and reflective, meaning-making processes is important, because the executive network draws from the products of the default network's reflections, and the default network reflects on what the executive network has paid attention to. In short, they feed each other.

All good so far, except that the default network activates when the executive network deactivates; we only turn inward to reflect when we stop focusing attention outward. The problem is, we don't deactivate very much these days. We are increasingly outward-focused, overloading the executive network and not allowing enough time for unstructured reflection, much to the alarm of the neuroscientists working in this field.[11] This is both a result of the constant "doing" that takes place in our overloaded schedules, as well as the pervasive role of technology in our lives (remember, the executive network loves technology, because it's full of stimuli). Constantly stimulating the executive network, however, crowds out the reflective cognitive processes of the default network. Without this, the cross talk and mutual functionality between the two processes is weakened.

Not reflecting has cognitive, social, emotional, and even moral consequences. That may seem like a bold statement, but neuroscientists are increasingly looking at the need for the use and development of the default network for increasing skills in managing conflict and emotions.[12] Without developed, creative, imaginative processes, we lose the ability to empathize, which is really just being able to imagine stepping into someone else's shoes, seeing their point of view, and imagining how they feel about things. Without those same creative processes applied to self, we follow rote patterns. Reflecting on what has happened, and imagining different future scenarios, is the antidote to pattern. It's how we leap into new possibilities for ourselves and the situations we are in.

One way to understand this is by showing what happens when these processes are interrupted. People suffering from PTSD, for example, show curtailed imaginative processes in waking time and are unable to access specific earlier memories from their life that contain nontraumatic emotions and experiences. Stuck in the traumatic event at night, their dreams tend toward a literal replaying of them. Interventions that center on reengaging imaginative processes reduce PTSD symptoms. As these symptoms diminish, night dreams begin to contain more bizarre, nonliteral elements as well as specific memories of other past emotional events. This opening-up of the imagination, and the emotional regulation and consolidation that happens in normally functioning sleep processes, allows the person to imagine beyond the traumatic event to new emotional expressions and ways of viewing their world.[13]

Creativity and imagination are critical for shifting our waking life experiences. Being able to *see* an emotion, for example, allows us to access it. Dream researcher Ernest Hartmann, whose work has included research with trauma victims, suggests that the image of overwhelming emotion in a dream (a tsunami, for example) can be mapped to earlier memories and information for finding a resolve, such as the idea of calming a wave.[14] This mapping, and the proposal of other memories and new ideas, is generated through the default network.

For all of us, not only do dreams give form to feeling, but by presenting an emotional perspective they open up a host of other possible perspectives. In an example from my own work, a client came to a session complaining about a months-long disagreement with her partner. In her dream, rather than appearing as a bad guy, the partner appeared in a suit made of shining jewels. As we worked with the dream, she listed the positive aspects he brings to the relationship—the jewels—and in doing so became aware of her own tendency to dismiss them. The disagreement, it turns out, wasn't the concrete subject of discussion, but rather her inability to see the value in the position he brought to the table. The conflict around the discussion wasn't *between* them, but *in* her; once this was realized, a total shift occurred both in her inner experience and the discussion with her partner.

Life moves fast, and we are often not aware of how we feel about something until after we've reacted to it. Seeing how we feel, we can calm our emotions, and we can also imagine other ways of responding. What is experienced in waking time as conflict may be opened out in dreaming such that we see a scenario altogether differently, thereby shifting what is possible in our next waking day. But in order to access this inner superpower contained within our default network, we need reflective, unstructured time, including ample time to sleep.

Scientists studying the default network point to technology use as a great disrupter in engaging it, as well as in developing its partnering work with the executive network. This is a very similar story as that of the neuroscientists who study sleep and dreams and decry the use of technology as being a main cause of modern sleep deprivation.[15] Lack of sleep on its own disturbs emotional regulation, cognition, and other biological functioning, and is deleterious to our mental and emotional health.[16] Very simply, we can think of the fussy toddler who needs a nap, or the equally fussy sleep-deprived adult who is easily triggered in a meeting as a result. Lack of sleep also leads to less dreaming time.

No matter where we turn, the data is clear: ample sleep and ample daydreaming time when awake are critical to our individual well-being, creative and cognitive functioning, and social relationships. Equally clear is that technology is the primary impediment to us getting enough of both. The problem is that technology is integrated into our lives. What to do?

Prepping for Dreams with a Pause

Technology becomes a problem when boundaries are not set around the use of it. Reflection needs empty space—time to look out the window and drift as we did in elementary school. Dreaming is no different. If we want to receive new ideas and the messages of our dreams, we have to make room for them. One way of doing so is through creating a practice around dreaming, which begins with a pause between technology and other stimulating activities and sleep.

Just as reflection requires a shift in focus—turning in instead of directing our attention outward—dreaming moves us from attending to external stimulation to attending to internal processes. We go from bustling activity to quieting; we even change our posture from vertical to horizontal, which is a perceptual shift from active to receptive. Making this transition intentional makes it a fertile time for reflection.

There's another place where transitioning is key, which is that from sleep to wake. Allowing oneself to remain in the transition space of sleep to wake is a highly fruitful time for reflecting on the content of our dreams and the many ideas that present themselves in this space. Think of this as a time for nourishing the work of the default network. Not only is this the time that we can more consciously play in the meaning-making of our dreams, it is also an intensely fertile space for reflective cognition.

Much of my personal creative work, including the writing of this book, happens in that space of "no-thinking" thought. Instead of trying to figure something out, insights are received. Think about how many times you've had a novel thought while in the shower. This unfocused, relaxed space is richly creative.

August Kekulé discovered the strange, circular chemical shape of the benzyne ring in just this way, relaxing into his fireside chair after having struggled with formulas to no avail. Lapsing into a reverie or doze, he saw the atoms playing and forming a long line that became a snake eating its tail. He leapt up and, with this new insight, immediately went back to his work and cracked the formula without anything distracting him from this ephemeral understanding.[17]

By contrast, Samuel Coleridge awoke with the whole of his famous work "Kubla Khan" in mind, but before he could write the poem in full a man knocked at his door, scattering his thoughts, and leaving the poem unfinished[18]—the ancient equivalent of a dinging phone notification. It's a good idea, therefore, to set technology aside for a few minutes on both sides of sleep, so that this abundant resource is fully utilized.

Pausing is easy and requires as little, or as much, time as works for you. The objective is to make a little space to change gears and turn your intention toward dreaming. It's a time to cultivate your own curiosity about yourself, your bigger picture beyond that day, and upon waking, to explore the sensations, images, and inner knowing that your dreams evoke.

You will find that the practice of pausing is revelatory in and of itself. Very often, it is the pause of an initial session with me that has marked impact for a client, before we even get to creating a practice of dreaming. New clients often say: "This is the first time in months I've actually had time to think about this," "I've never taken the time to put this into words," or "I guess I never stopped long enough to ask myself these questions." These statements speak to what happens in the pause. The mind turns away from goals and lists to look inward and to go below the surface of things. From this deceptively simple act of stepping out of the hurricane of busy life, the inner waters clear, revealing possibility like the glittering scales of a silver fish. Simply by virtue of pausing and disengaging a bit from daily noise, emotions, and expectations, my clients begin to solve their own problems by seeing what they couldn't see before. They begin to dream their life again.

The Dreaming Practice

Every neuroscientist who studies dreams will tell you that simple encouragement to remember dreams increases dream recall.[19] Remember that in the study James Pagel conducted on people who said they never dreamed, many began dreaming *after* participating in the study. Most of my clients, and even people with whom I am scheduled to have just a regular work meeting, remember a dream before meeting me. The idea of meeting a dreamer jogs their mind and stimulates their dream recall. Dreams are remembered if we turn our attention to them. This means getting curious about them, perhaps even deciding that dreams are important. I'll go so far as to say that it means deciding that the inner life is important and getting curious about that. Opening to the possibility that dreams relate specifically to our lives, that they are, perhaps, letters to the Self that contain a message, begins the relationship with dreaming. Like any relationship, this initial choice to be curious leads to a greater unfolding of it.

A dream practice begins by getting a dream journal and writing your dreams every single night. How we write them, and what we write, however, makes a difference to the practice. We have to record the full details of the visceral experience; every detail is important. You'll see how much this is true as we continue along in how we work with dreams themselves.

First, get a fresh journal. Find one that you really love, enjoy looking at and touching, and makes you excited by the blank pages of possibility that await within. Make it dedicated to this new practice you are engaging in—set apart, not a scrap of paper found somewhere nearby or a notepad used for something else. Intent moves us to change.

Having found the journal, the next step is to set the nightly intention. Do it each night before going to bed by writing on the first blank page of the journal the day's date and the sentence: "Tonight I will have a Clear Dream and remember it" (more on Clear Dreams in Chapter Six). Put your pen in place, ready to record what arrives.

At this point, the first question my clients ask me is about using their phone; they think it will be easier to speak or type into their Notes app than it is to write. In addition to breaking the no-technology buffer, the cognitive engagement that occurs when opening a phone pulls us out of the unfocused reverie of dream. The habitual use of phones for news, work, and social conversations immediately puts us into the mode of thinking about daily, waking activities. Each of these things makes it harder to remember the details of our dreams. Dreams need to be captured right away, without changing location. In this space, the details are "right there" and active, and we are still in the default mode of processing that will aid our sense-making of the dream.

Additionally, there is much to mine in the actual way in which dreams are written. Our dreamy handwriting will often instinctively underline a word, sketch an image, or phrase something in an unusual way. The specific ways in which we spell (and misspell) words, the words themselves, and how they are positioned—interposed, on top of each other, sometimes accompanied by drawings or symbols—often contain the most telling and useful aspects of the dream.

These aspects are either not able to be captured at all by devices, or they are autocorrected. We usually don't pay attention to these automatic corrections in our sleepy state. Returning to the dream later, we don't remember what it was we were trying to say; the gems of the puns and pointed "errors" of the dream are lost. The best dream engagement, therefore, is with an old-fashioned journal and pen, made even better because of its distinction from our regular way of recording something. We seek something new and different in our dreaming; to catch it, we use something new and different.

Now let's turn to *what* we write. Everything that is remembered is to be written, just as it is remembered, with no editing. Even if what is remembered is only a fragment, it is written down. A color, a scent, a feeling, a snippet of a song—one single image—any and all of these are dreams. Write them down fully. If you wake up more than once in the night with dreams, write them all down—every dream had in one night is one dream.

That seems easy enough; however, the simple act of writing a dream in all the remembered details, just as they appear, sheds light on our tendency to edit and limit ourselves. When I work with a client and ask questions to clarify the details of a dream, they often add numerous elements to what they had originally written down. When I ask why they hadn't included these details before, they tell me things like: "I didn't think that was important," "that wasn't really a dream so I didn't think it mattered," "that part didn't make any sense to me so I didn't include it," or "I was embarrassed (or afraid) to put that part in."

The tendency to edit dreams is a signpost of our relationship with change, level of flexibility, and ability to hear, ponder, and experience something new and unknown. Just as with pausing, part of the *practice* of a dreaming practice is developing the capacity for change, fluidity, and mystery. Simply learning to see, without judgment, whatever arises from within us is to learn to face ourselves fully in the mirror. Emotions without judgment can be shifted; thoughts and belief systems without judgment can be evaluated, chosen, or discarded. If we are unwilling to see them as they are, we'll never be able to transform them; we cannot change that which we are denying. Writing every aspect of what is remembered of a dream—without any editing, assumptions, or criticism—teaches us to see the world for what it is, as well as learn to see something new.

The expectations and assumptions we build of the world ensure that this is all the world we will ever experience. What we expect to see, we see—the image freezes. Plans are made, and outcomes are controlled for. This is part of our propensity for error—when new information appears that doesn't fit these constructed frames, it is dismissed or suppressed. Seeing in this blinkered way, one is often confused by people's actions, wondering what went wrong in a discussion or job, or stumped as to why things didn't turn out as wanted. The same error is made when seeing our inner world through expectation. Suppressing a thought, an image, an emotion not only holds us back from our self-discovery, it leaves us in an unintegrated state, where decisions are predetermined or unable to be made, and actions are taken that we don't understand. Allowing ourselves to feel and see what arises in dreams, without altering it to make it less intense, less frightening, or more or less exciting, builds a muscle of change.

The "out-of-the-blue" quality of the material in dreams that "doesn't make sense" to the linear mind operates entirely outside mental constructs, creating space for true revelation; it's this "absurd" element that is often the most important aspect of the dream.

For the woman at the top of the chapter who wanted to work in writing and the arts, this idea was—to the awake linear mind—a complete absurdity; if it were rational, she would have already quit her current job and done it. We all know the many reasons that we can find to tell ourselves that change isn't possible. This is why sleep is such an important aspect of the dreaming process. Here the dreamer is fully receptive and able to be caught by surprise, and therefore able to explore the so-called absurd.

Pulling us out of the ordered, comfortable, patterned character of daily life, dreams place us in new worlds and scenarios that engage our senses, emotions, physical movements, and sense of space and time in both recognized and new ways, which automatically enlarges our perspectives.[20] These richly visceral experiences wake us up to something in our inner world, challenging our points of view with unexpected images, perspectives, and sensations, disrupting complacency via question. The woman seeking to work in writing and the arts quite literally experienced the juxtaposition of the lugubrious plodding of a horse and carriage to the energetic zipping of a modern speedboat in her dream. This one sensory experience unleashed further questions: *How many feelings in life are available beyond tired, bored, distracted, or drained? Why am I waiting to live my dream of Self? Why am I waiting to feel energetic and zippy?*

The dramatic experience of dream opens us to a place of imagination and sensation that opposes the safe choice of now. These visceral experiences become a new destination. It doesn't matter if that destination can be defined in detail: *What job in the arts? Writing about what?* The "feeling" of the dream experience is evident, and the possibility of it is deeply understood in an embodied way. Daily life, colorless and routine, is shaken up by the body's reconnection to sensation and the thrill of inner passion. After this, the details—*Which job? How?* —take care of themselves when moving from the new energy of the dream.

It is for this reason that every detail must be captured when writing our dreams, including bodily sensations, and all the aspects which, at first glance, don't seem to make sense. Remaining in the space of feeling while writing a dream retains the physical experience and inner knowing the dream provokes. Staying with this body-based, inner knowing cultivates the potency to continue in this space of possibility and begin to move in new directions.

Writing down dreams documents the imaginative experiences of our inner world and brings us closer to admitting, and therefore realizing, our inner passions. The act of writing a dream is a direct engagement with the Self; by putting it on paper, the dream is brought into a tangible reality, making the inner imaginings of the Self real and important. This concrete acknowledgement of our inner world brings it into the external world where manifestation occurs.

The Rav Chisda quote that opened this chapter compares an unexamined dream to a letter that one does not open. We are so much more than we perceive ourselves to be. Establishing a dream practice opens the letters of our inner world, launching us on an exploration of our greater Self.

The next step of working with dreams takes us even further in that journey. It starts with understanding the images of dreams: where they come from and how to understand them. So let's turn now to imagery in dreams.

CHAPTER TWO

The Language of Experience

"Once upon a time, I dreamt I was a butterfly. . . . Now I do not know whether I was then a man dreaming I was a butterfly, or whether I am now a butterfly, dreaming I am a man."

—ZHUANGZI, Chinese philosopher[1]

A woman comes to me faced with a decision: a job offer from two equally impressive companies. How to choose? The decision had left her frozen for days. In our session, we do a waking dream exercise. She closes her eyes, and in her mind, she sees ahead of her an almond tree, with one single golden almond hanging from it. Her eyes pop open and she tells me that her choice is not to take *either* job offer, but to take the almond. It's what she's always wanted to do but never had the courage to say: She wants to start her own company.

How can a single image be so provocative that it incites us to make a life-changing decision?

Experience and Form

The entire human experience is one of physical form. Our thoughts, our sense of self, our notion of soul or consciousness is housed within the form of our own physical body and made real by it.[2] Everything that we know comes from our experience of being in our physical body and from the experience of that physical body interacting in a physical world. We cannot separate ourselves from our physical experience of form, and in fact, it is this physical experience that *creates* that very sense of self and understanding of the world.

Images are physical forms. They are the building blocks of our understanding of everything we call experience or thought. We struggle to understand a math problem using symbols for height, depth, and width until the teacher draws a picture on the board: a simple visual of a swimming pool making clear the dimensions of height, depth, and width that we are using in the problem. Suddenly we "see," and seeing is tangible understanding.[3]

Beyond algebra, we understand all of life's experiences through the form of image. The inscrutable inner world of another person is made known through the image they make with their body, forming a smile and opening arms wide, or closing in, grimacing, and raising fists.[4] Abstract notions such as a sense of creation, or a universal force greater than ourselves, are brought into reach by images of the Milky Way or a grand waterfall. The same goes for ideas such as possibility, or its opposite, which we may understand by viewing an unrestricted horizon or seeing a tiny box.

In addition to understanding experiences through external images, for every experience we have there is also an image formed within us that tells us about that experience.[5] These images come from our bodies, and we can see them in our mind's eye. They give us something substantial to grab on to, like a mirror's reflection, something to orient us as to where we are, what is going on, how we feel about it, and what we know as a result. They are the meeting point of our outer and inner experiencing.

Let's say I feel my heart pounding, blood rising to my face, and hear a rushing sound in the ears upon meeting someone. My thinking self may not yet have discerned if this is "love" or "anxiety," or even something else. "Love" and "anxiety" are words we use, but in fact they are as abstract as the symbols the math teacher puts on the board. My body-brain, however, will have formed an image of this experience so that I can visualize and understand it. Maybe it is an image of a sparkling fountain, which I understand as love. It could also be an image of a room with the walls closing in, which I connect to anxiety. These two very different images help make clear what is happening. Because image is something we can see and has a sense of materiality and realness to it, it makes our inner, subjective world real and tangible.

These inner images are present throughout our waking day, even though most of us aren't aware of them. They are, for the most part, precognitive and preverbal, bubbling at the base of our experiencing, though we can learn to become aware of them, which you will do in this book. The default network we began discussing in previous chapters is image-based. Meaning, all its cognitive work is done via image, not what we typically think of as "thoughts." We tend to associate "thoughts" with words and verbal communication, but verbal communication comes *after* image and is in large part simply describing the images we are experiencing, whether or not we are conscious to the process. We may say to someone, "This idea feels like a dead end," for example, without realizing that we have an inner image of exactly that: a dead end. And yet, it is the dead end image in our mind's eye that *gave* us the inner understanding that we verbalize. Before the image, we didn't know how we felt about the idea; the image informed us of that knowing. Images, in other words, answer the question: *How do I know what I know?*

Dreams are composed of images. We can say that images are the "words" that make up the "sentences" of dreams. These images come from the same mechanism as the images we find in our mind's eye in the daytime, but we see the images of dreams more easily, because in sleep we are no longer distracted by the busy activity of our waking day. Instead of looking out and moving forward, we lay back and tune in to our inner screen. Here we get the "story behind the story" of what we are experiencing in the day, organized in a kind of narrative so that we can make sense of it.

I say that we "lay back" and "tune in," but dreams physically move us every bit as much as a movie, if not more. We might pant, sweat, feel our heart pounding, or fear or desire something in our dreams. We might cry as if we were watching a sad movie or have an energetic, muscular adventure like we're in an action film. We might feel like we are exploding with anger, or we may even orgasm with pleasure. Just as the images of day are associated with sensory, physical, and emotional experiences, so, too, are the images of our dreams.

The physical and emotional provocations of images communicate information like a bullet point in a presentation, just differently. We know if we are shaking or frozen or hot or explosive that *something* is happening, and we know that there is a difference between each of these experiences. We know, for example, that "explosive" is not having a serene day with friends and that "frozen" is not giving an awesome speech. We may also recognize a sensation and remember it from another time, like freezing in first grade when asked a question in front of the class. This memory gives us an additional layer of understanding. Combine all of this with the visual component of image and we have a very complete comprehension of what is actually happening to us in the moment.

Inner images speak to our present tense, bringing us back to "right now." Emotions, feelings, and the load of information in any given moment may take us off track, sending our thoughts away from our embodied sense of presence. Return to our inner images, though, and we can see to sort through it all. More importantly, we can see whether we are blocked or fluid, and we can figure out what our blocks are.

Images also bring into view a larger array of possibilities available to us—new perspectives, new scenarios. These we surely miss if we are deep in an emotional reaction or acting in a familiar or patterned way. In dream, we get to explore these perspectives, process these emotions, understand our waking time, and problem-solve our blocks. This cognitive work of images helps us make meaning of events and imagine future possibilities that will help us grow and develop our potentials.

Because the body is always making images to speak to us about what we are experiencing, we can say that we are dreaming all the time, night and day. Both use the same neurobiological processing system of the default network. This is one of the fundamental points on which this books rests: dreaming and waking are two sides of one experiential coin. This is key for our learning how to use dreaming as a transformative tool.

Tuning into our inner screen, unlike the passive experience of watching a movie, is an active engagement. We not only live out the scenario, we *are* the scenario, which means we can change it. This is another of the fundamental points of this book: not only are our inner images speaking to us, we also get to dialogue back. Understanding that we are at once the playwright, director, actors, and stage itself gives us numerous spaces to intervene and change the aspects that aren't working for us. This is when we become conscious agents in the creation of our lives. This intervention can take place by working with night dreams, or with inner images of waking time. While we may not be in the habit of seeing our inner images in waking time, we can learn to do so.

At the top of the chapter, I describe an imagery exercise wherein a woman sees a single almond tree with a single golden almond hanging from it. This imagery exercise was a way of seeing and interacting with these inner images, what I call dreaming awake. She closed her eyes, and I used a short verbal prompt to get her to return to this dreaming-awake, image-based cognition. That one image told her everything she needed to know about what she needed to do. While the thinking mind had her lost in a quagmire of pros and cons, lists, and conflicting advice from others, her body—via image—plugged her straight into her greatest inner vision and evoked all the sense-based information and memories that brought it alive for her. When we stop thinking in words and start thinking in images, we tune in to the part of ourselves that is literally showing us the bigger picture of all that we are perceiving, sensing, feeling, and knowing.

Because images are the building blocks of all this inner dialogue, to speak the language of dreams, we must speak image. It's a language we all already know and simply have to remember. We start by going to the origin of image, which is in our bodies.

Making Images

Our entry as humans into this world is an explosion of physical sensations. First breath and we begin to take the world in, building a database of experience, adding to it all the information we are getting though our tasting, seeing, smelling, hearing, touching, and moving, and the tremendous amount of learning that this sensual-physical interaction promotes. Like astronauts in a skinsuit, we use the gates of our senses, and physical movement, to take samples of this strange new planet.[6] Each sense impression, and mobile experience is data about the world we've landed in and how it works.

Let's take trees as an example. We come to know trees not only by seeing them, but by also interacting with them on a sense level. We pull a crisp pear or apple off a branch and crunch into it. We sit under branches and hear the rustling sound of wind blowing leaves, catch the sharp smell of sap, and feel the solidity of a trunk at our backs with sunlight filtering through high branches to touch our skin.

This interaction is not just a one-way, data-gathering exercise—we also have a response to each of these experiences. We may register the crisp pear as fresh and new, the rustling wind as rattling and nervous, the sharp sap as invigorating, and the sunlight touching our skin as an expanded sensation. We may look up at the tree and feel a sense of awe at its height. That awe we feel may incur a sense of respect—we may even step back a bit. We may register the rattle of the rustling wind as unpleasant; we may record the expanded sensation of the sunlight as soothing.

As we make our sense-based exploration of tree, these interactions also have a cognitive component. It is through embodiment that we not only feel, but also learn and know.[7] Perhaps we've chosen a tree with a thick trunk that is deeply rooted. Feeling that and comparing our mobile human body against the thick and rooted tree body, we learn about solidity and develop an idea of grounding. The tree's "there" and our "anywhere" establishes a contrast between being rooted and stable and of moving toward endless new impressions. Maybe we climb the tree but don't get all the way to the treetop disappearing from view into the bright sun above, stopping ourselves when we sense the threat of gravity pulling us down if we fall.

Climbing up, falling down, things within and out of reach, the desire for height, a fear of falling, the idea that ground is comforting and height is dizzying—all of these experience and sense-based understandings become entries in our database, along with the deep understandings they confer, stretching far beyond one interaction with a tree. They lay a larger foundation about how the world is structured.

In our adult state, where much of our work and thought is seemingly abstract, it is easy to forget the intense experiences of our sensual exploration of the world and the role this plays in developing who we are and what we know. It's impossible to read the exploration with tree, however, without hearing common adult phrases in it: "feeling grounded," "climbing up to a higher level." Physical and sense-based understandings become abstracted into adult language and goals. Though we tend to "think that we think," what we understand as thinking is generated from physical, sense-based experience. How many times have you described your next goal as "just within reach"? The first understanding of that experience happened before you had acquired verbal language, perhaps as you stretched toward the curious object in the mobile hanging above your crib.[8]

The totality of our experiences—the entries in our database—write a personal encyclopedia containing our knowledge of Self and world. This understanding is intensely subjective. It's not just *any* tree we interact with, but a specific one, in a specific moment. Perhaps we think of a special tree we climbed and hid behind each summer on a family camping trip, or a tree we planted and watched grow from sapling to shade-bearing in our yard. These specific experiences, and our bodily responses to them, also become part of our image repertoire.

Our lived experiences, and the particular sensations, memories, and knowledge of these experiences become the unique images of our inner dialogue. This uniqueness is part of what makes our inner images and dreams so meaningful. Composed of the data we've been collecting since our first moments on the planet, they are not only our body's way of dialoguing with us, they also help us shape ourselves into who we are.

In our own bodies we can't ever see ourselves physically in full—it takes a system of mirrors to see the back of our body, which is still only glimpsed in small slices that we put together to form a whole. In the same way, the interaction with the world outside, with its myriad aspects, informs us of our own myriad aspects. We develop our sense of self and world through an exploration of the many other forms around us, encountering, comparing, and contrasting, like with our tree exercise. We have experiences, we learn from them, we like or don't like them, and we do something with them, or not. Maybe we take a big risk and climb to the top of the tree; maybe we are stymied by such a risk and stay on a low branch. Each interaction is one reflection from a single mirror; through many reflections, something of a whole develops of our concept of both the world and the Self.

The client I describe at the top of the chapter had an inner image of an almond tree, with a golden almond, which signaled her heart's desire of opening her own practice. When she saw this image, she said to me that she could *smell* and *taste* the tree and the almond. She described these sensations as exciting and reminiscent of the almond trees of her childhood when she was "free, running and playing." My client understood that childhood moment in a very specific way: excitement, freedom, and play. Which means she understood what her inner self was telling her now, as an adult, in showing the almond tree and provoking those same feelings. Her heart's desire to open her own practice was freedom, and her inner self knew this was the right choice for her.

Images speak to us, personally, in ways that we understand. Not only do we recognize the image, we are viscerally and emotionally moved in some way upon seeing it. This means that we understand not only its multidimensional message, but also its importance. That physical sensation translates into an emotion and a desire to act[9] —we like it, we discard it, we step back, we step in, and so on.

For my client, sensations of freedom, running, and playing prompted a life change. Images truly are worth more than a thousand words; they are also extremely powerful. As any artist (and neuroscientist) knows, we change behavior not by our minds, but by our hearts.[10]

Notice that in addition to the almond tree, and the sense-based memory of it, my client also saw a single, golden almond. This was not part of the childhood experience—it was something extraordinarily different. And yet, it was part of the dialogue of the inner image. In fact, it was the main message, which the sensation of freedom underlined.

Inner images draw upon the database of experience, but they then combine information in new ways. It is this newness of the spontaneous imagination that makes it a true dialogue, rather than just a static memory recall. We can think of this like a verbal vocabulary; while there may be a finite set of words, we can combine them into infinite new sentences. The ability to imagine infinite new combinations is what safeguards our evolution; without it, we would arrive at one idea in an early stage of learning, or come upon one challenge and get stuck, and just stay there. Because we are innately creative vis-à-vis our spontaneous imagination, we can always transform.[11]

Image and Action

From the point of view of cognitive psychology, our inner images are our most basic unit of thought and cognition.[12] Image is our blueprint for understanding and action.[13] What we see in our mind's eye is what stirs our physical body, elicits emotion, and determines behavior. In a very simple way, we can understand that when I turn on my car, if I don't have an image in my mind of where I aim to go,

I won't put the car in gear and drive. I have to first have an image of "grocery store," or "work" as a destination to move toward. This holds, even if in my image I see a block.

When my client saw the golden almond, she also said, "There's just this box in the way between me and it." Because image determines action, the block of the box meant that my client was unable to move forward in her decision-making. Either she would remain stuck or find a way to overcome it.

Reading image, we can look at my client's experience and understand that the box was the image of the obstacle that had caused her to book a session with me. That one little image was the forty-five minutes of circular deliberation that took place during the first part of the session, a block "hidden in plain sight." Incredibly, in our session, my client never mentioned that she had ever thought of her own practice. This one box, generating forty-five minutes of words that went nowhere, kept us from getting there, even though that was what really needed to be discussed. Also, neither of us ever said the word "box" in our conversation. But you see—the "box" was in fact all we discussed. It was the thing getting in the way of her doing what she already knew, deep down inside, that she wanted to do.

Because images are the locus of understanding and action, that means the box had to shift for her to move forward. To do that, I had her close her eyes again and see in her mind's eye a return to the image. I then prompted her to find a way over or around or through the box to get to the almond. Suddenly she said, "Oh! It was just a cardboard box—I hopped over it and the almond was immediately there."

We overcome our blocks by interacting with our inner images in the same spontaneous way that they interact with us. Rather than scripting something or fantasizing about what we *want* to happen, we simply enter into the dialogue in a responsive manner. If there's a box, and the need is to get to the golden almond, one can just return to the image and do something with the box. Working this way stays within the spontaneous imagination, which will then shift and move in response. This is what happened when my client discovered that the box was not insurmountable, but merely cardboard.

On the surface of things, life seems full of rational decision-making. We carefully consider options, and like my client, we produce long lists of pros and cons that are composed of what—externally, at least—makes sense. This kind of thinking, though, is causal: A leads to B. That means it is also linear, like a chain, with one thought "rationally" leading to another; for example, this promotion sets me up for the next one. And yet, for all that logical thinking, my client couldn't take a decision until she dipped inside and reconnected with the image that contained her true understanding of her situation. Rational reasoning left her confused. When she reconnected with her inner image and the *bodily* experience of it, however, the knowing was clear, and the decision was instant. Rather than continuing the current trajectory of her life as part of a causal, linear chain, she leaped into something entirely new. And yet, the leap was *perfectly sensible* in her inner knowing.

Logical thinking and experience are two different means of cognition.[14] Both are valid, and we use them every day. But logical thinking and experience are processed completely differently. This means that we can't use logical thinking to extract meaning from the images that come of experience. We really do have to read and speak image. It isn't about asking *Why a box?*, but is instead about *interacting* with the box—or any other image—in the way it appears. Part of what helps us do that is focusing in on the sensation of it. The felt sensation of the box was clear—it was blocking movement. Experiential cognition is deeply embodied; we "know that we know" because of how images move our bodies. To truly speak image, then, we have to be in the experience of it. If we jump out of the experience of images to try to "make sense" of them using logical thought, we lose their sense, as well as lose our ability to make a change in our lives right then and there.[15]

Our bodies, and the experiential cognition of images, are always present tense. This means that as sensing, acting organisms our bodies are oriented toward active response. Dialoguing with our body's inner images is very quick; its sense of knowing very clear. It's our logical mind that is often patterned and stifling of an experience that slows us down. My client had spent days in stagnant deliberation over her decision—all that rational thought that resulted in so much wasted time and energy. Thankfully, we can cut to the chase by looking inside to see what our inner images are telling us. In this internal space, the forty-five-minute "box" was "*just* a cardboard box" and it was leaped over in one second. The total time of the dreaming awake exercise took less than two minutes for her to find her inner truth, overcome the mental obstruction blocking her from freely accessing it, and move forward.

Once we click into our inner knowing, then we can plug back into our logical thinking to know how to execute the new plan. The default network (the part that thinks in image) and the executive network (the one that focuses on goals and tasks) work together, with information from each feeding the other. Once my client got the picture (literally) she immediately ended the session because she wanted to go right away to an office space she had seen that might be right for her practice.

Logical-rational thinking is meant to work in tandem with experiential knowing. As adults, however, we tend to put the cart before the horse, trying to think our way through things before first becoming aware of what we feel, know, and understand about the experience. The more we connect with the image language of our present-tense experiencing, the more we do what is right for us. We stop losing time deliberating, circling, or setting aside vital aspects of our individual experience.

My client unblocked a hidden passion. Releasing this block gave her back a tremendous amount of energy that became the engine that drove her to do what she needed to do to start her practice and see success. Within three months she was billing so much that she was on track to make more than either of the two other offers had proposed, and she was already hiring associates. She was doing what she loved, providing for her family at the same time, and she was excited, motivated, and having fun with life. A golden almond, indeed.

Speaking Image

The first step in speaking image, and subsequently in making change in our lives, is to use the present tense. Start by writing your dreams in the present tense. "I am" feels, and is, different than "I was." Notice what shifts in your relationship to your dreams by bringing them to your right-now. Choose one and read it out loud later in the day and pay attention to how it feels in your body hearing it in the present tense.

We cultivate our capacity to speak image by putting our focus on sensation and experience and developing our vocabulary to describe it. The second step, then, is to slip back into the physical sensation of image and the way it moves the body. Verbally describing these sensations connects us back to our inner experience, especially when we remember to use present tense. The more detailed we can be in our description, the more present we are to it, and the more we expand our ability to experience.

One way to practice this is to begin to pay attention to what you are experiencing in different moments and describe these experiences to yourself in all their details. Pick a moment you do often, like getting your coffee in the morning, and slow it down—what is happening in your body? As you walk outside at the end of the workday, what is your body experiencing? Bodies expand and contract, toes wiggle, little starts of silvery electricity shimmer up our backs. We light up or feel we've stepped into a shadow; our shoulders tense or relax, and so much more. Be as detailed as possible in your descriptions. You may even want to carry a notebook for this, to capture these experiences and descriptions.

It helps to also explore the natural world in the same descriptive fashion. Nature is the mirror to human experience. There we find the qualities in our own selves that we describe, such as the rooted tree we mentioned earlier. Describing the myriad facets you find in nature is to discover the myriad facets in yourself. When they show up as images in your dreams, you'll have a breadth of experience to understand them.

All this discussion of how we form images leads us to a foundational aspect of how we work with dreams: **Every aspect of the dream is an aspect of the dreamer.** A tree in a dream is an aspect of the one who is dreaming it. Realizing this helps us to explore different expressions of our energy and find within them new perspectives and possibilities—like a golden almond.

No single one of us will ever have exactly the same experience; all of us will develop our own completely unique inner images. One person's childhood experience playing under almond trees creates an inner language of feeling, out of which, around the question of starting their own business, appears a single golden almond. Another person sees a red motorboat zipping down the River Seine. Both understand their image as a decision to do something new.

The subjective component of dreams means that one-size-fits-all approaches to dreams never work. Neither dream dictionaries that look at images as symbols, nor lists of metaphors and archetypes that corral experience into preset constructs are effective in dream work. Cognitive linguists have tried to map metaphoric structures to dreams, but with no success[16] for this very reason. Dream dictionaries, metaphors, and archetypes are generalized; images are not.

As subjective as our inner experience may be, though, we share with all humans the experience of being in a physical body in a physical existence. Regardless of how unique the specific images are to each dream and dreamer, they are undergirded by universal structures deriving from, and specific to, physical experience, like gravity, something we all know and hold in common.

The physicality of our bodies and the world we live in structure our dreams, grounding them in what I call the physical laws of dreaming.[17] These laws derive from embodiment—how we move in space and time, and what we know and understand from these movements. One example is spatial relationships, such as height. We discovered in our exploration with trees that we have certain embodied understandings of rising up and falling down; too high can become ungrounded, which is remedied by rooting down. That physical law is then detailed by a specific experience—am I, right now, rooted or picking up roots to move my family to a new town and new opportunity? My image will show me. Knowing the universal, physical law of rooted or not, and then seeing the specific contextual image of my interaction with it, is what allows me to dialogue with that experience.

The particular component of images is what makes our dream unique to us; the universal component of our shared physical experience is what makes us able to hear the dream of another person and understand it. One person may have a golden almond, but all of us have experienced freedom and play. The language of images is universal. Through image, not only can we understand another's experience, by doing so we learn something about our own self. This shared language means that we can even dream together of a future we wish to create.

Now that you know how to speak image, our next step is to look at entire dreams, which is where we go in the next chapter.

CHAPTER THREE

Nightmare or Wonder? Seven Different Kinds of Dreams

"I'm in a car that's going way too fast. It's dark, we can barely see the road. So many people are crammed in the car, and the music is turned up so loud. Suddenly I see there's a giant, gaping hole in the road up ahead. There's no way we can stop in time—we're going to fall in!"

—DREAMER

We know them by the way they shake our bodies, terrifying us at night, and stalking us in peripheral resonances throughout the day.

Nightmares.

They have dark colors we struggle to see through clearly, black hues and the red of blood and explosions. In Nightmares our bodies don't respond to our will, moving too slowly or too fast. The world of Nightmares is out of control.

The dream I excerpted at the top of the chapter is clearly a Nightmare. The dreamer reported waking up "in a sweat," having "thrashed around in the sheets," her heart "pounding." The dream is dark, hard to see, and has a looming terror. But there are other kinds of dreams that awaken us in surprise or delight. Sometimes we have a dream that changes our life.

Just as we have different dream experiences, we have different kinds of life experiences. A night out with friends, for example, is not the same as a confrontation with a boss. One is fun, the other contentious, anxious, or angry. With friends the pace is leisurely and smooth; confrontation, however, is fast and choppy. The experience with friends we remember in detail, with vivid colors and other sensations—like what people were wearing, what someone ordered on the menu, how a certain dish tasted. The experience of the confrontation with the boss remains a blur, hard to recall clearly, and barely seen the first time through. We might even say, "I just saw red."

In the same way that we can describe distinctly different waking experiences with their unique qualities, so, too, can we describe the different qualities of our dreams and sort them into distinct kinds.[1]

There are seven different kinds of dreams:

- Nightmare
- Repetitive Nightmare
- Busy Dream
- Clear Dream
- Great Dream
- Light Dream
- Dreams of Union

This chapter explores the seven kinds of dreams. We'll look at examples of dreams my clients have had and their differences and similarities. We'll also take a look at how dreams relate to waking experience and vice versa. Understanding this is an important key for becoming present in our life and taking conscious charge of crafting the life we want to live. We're going to start by talking about Nightmares, Repetitive Nightmares, Busy Dreams, and Clear Dreams.

Nightmares

We learned in Chapter One that everyone dreams, even if they don't remember their dreams. Nightmares are perhaps the most commonly remembered dream. Nightmares are acute, frightening, and easy to recognize because of their physical intensity, which often wakes us up. The intense physical sensations they produce, and the terrifying images and situations that we find ourselves in, make a visceral and emotional impression on us. It's this physical and emotional intensity which causes us to remember them. We may try to forget these strong impressions and physical imprints, to "shake them off" as we would shudder while brushing past a cobweb or jerk away from a grasping hand. And yet, Nightmares stay with us, often haunting us throughout the day.

We can describe Nightmares as dark, composed of dark or disturbing colors—blacks, reds, maybe acid colors. In a Nightmare, we may have a sense of having no control; we may find our self or surroundings freezing, moving too fast, or moving too slow. Nightmares are often experienced as short in the sense of duration—as if they are just a clip of a film right at the moment of crisis.

Perhaps counterintuitively, Nightmares can be considered friendly messengers. They function as urgent, direct warnings, pressing signals that something is off balance in our body-world system. Their purpose is to wake us up both physically and cognitively, bringing to our attention something that needs to be seen and corrected in our life course.

Like a "first responder," Nightmares arrive on the scene of an error in progress: a conflict that has arisen between friends, a new challenge at work, an unexpected illness in the family. Their role in the first-aid kit is to tell us quickly where our energies have become tied up, knotted, and tangled—things that keep us from being able to respond to the issue and solve it. They point out where we've frozen or lashed out in the face of a challenge, where we've snarled our creative energies and left them locked in a box, or where we've shut off the lights in the room that contains something we don't want to see or face. They show us where we're ducking out of the theater before the movie even has time to start, or where we're running in a panic, moving so fast that "our car is out of control, and we no longer have hold of the steering wheel." In other words, Nightmares sound the alarm that our body is out of balance and that we are out of sync with ourselves.

Nightmares are usually simple and plain in meaning, with few characters or scenes. If we pay attention to them and engage with them, they are easily resolved. One way to do that is to interact directly with the Nightmare itself, using a method called the Waking Dream. I'll show you how to do that in a later chapter. There's also another way, which is to figure out where the block is in our waking time. If Nightmares are signaling something in our waking time that is out of balance, locating its origin puts us in position to resolve it.

To understand how Nightmares relate to waking life, an easy first step is to say out loud the situation of the Nightmare, as I've done in the paragraph above—"locked in a box," "frozen," "in the dark because of not wanting to see." This image or situation will likely resonate with something going on in your waking life. Hearing it said out loud helps make that connection. You might even recall having used an exact or similar phrase in talking about the situation to a friend, or in your own self-talk.

For example, one client I worked with shared a dream where she walks into a large stadium filled with lots of people. Somehow, she feels very angry at them. Suddenly, she realizes she is holding a huge flamethrower. To her horror, she blasts the entire stadium, setting everything on fire. Even though she doesn't want to, the flamethrower is more powerful than she is, and she can't stop blasting the flame. The situation of this Nightmare can be described as "blasting out in anger." Once the client said this out loud, the bridge between the Nightmare and waking life was apparent. The client told me that she was "mad at everything in my life right now. I just had no idea how much I was putting that on other people." The Nightmare woke her up to the ferocity of the anger she was experiencing—the flame-throwing—as well as its consequences, which was the blasting or lashing out that razed the whole stadium. This realization motivated her to address the issues in her life that were causing her to react in anger, which resolved the Nightmare, both in waking and sleep.

Resolving Nightmares restores balance in the body and frees up vital energies that were bound up in them. We usually don't realize how taxing emotional reactions to unresolved problems can be. Here is a little exercise: flex a muscle and hold it. How long can you do it? It takes a lot of energy and attention to do this. Likewise, it takes a lot of energy and attention to remain angry, grip onto tension, or experience any of the emotional reactions signaled by a Nightmare.

Energy is a finite resource. When our energy and attention are tied up in maintaining the situation of a Nightmare, we can't use them to creatively resolve it. Either we stay locked in emotional reaction, or we find a way to free ourselves to respond. Responding to the Nightmare to resolve it is like letting go of the muscle. As soon as we respond, energy returns to us. Then we can dream a different kind of dream.

Paying attention to Nightmares involves taking responsibility for them, facing the challenge, and actively resolving them. Often, however, we tend to run from them and the frightening or anxious feelings they arouse. We may pass them off as an unfortunate dream and hope for a better one in the coming night. We may tell ourselves they are meaningless—"just a dream"—even while we remain disturbed by the feelings they've elicited.

Some clients begin working with me after having used things like medication or alcohol in order to sleep a dreamless sleep, so fearful were they of what their dreams might be. Unfortunately, these substances deaden us to our natural tool for self-correction. One client came to me after three years of taking sleeping pills every night to avoid Nightmares. She told me that "dreams are meaningless," and yet she was so disturbed by what her inner world contained that she didn't even want to close her eyes for a corrective exercise in our session. We eventually worked with one dream that she remembered, and the next day she emailed me to say that she slept without sleeping pills and, for the first time in years, she had no Nightmares.

The thing to remember about Nightmares is that they are simple scenarios. They are acute, right-now messages: today there was an argument with a friend, or this afternoon my child got sick and I missed an important presentation. Because they are simple, and current, they are equally simple to resolve. These challenges don't seem simple, though, if we are having an emotional reaction to it. It's the emotional reaction, not the challenge, that instigated the Nightmare. This emotional reaction obscures our ability to see how simply we can intervene to change the situation and resolve the challenge. It may take a few conversations with the friend to resolve the argument, and the child may be sick for a couple of days, but if our angry, frozen, or panicked state is corrected then we will find fluid, harmonious, or creative ways of dealing with it.

The tendency to dismiss Nightmares is no different from the tendency to avoid confrontation, shy away from challenges that frighten us, or bury feelings and try to forget them. We think the challenge or emotional intensity is too much for us. And yet, all of us have all the tools we need to overcome these challenges, resolve the conflicts, and address our emotions in dreams and waking life. Those tools are found in our inner self, which is accessed by our inner images and dreams. They're already there, waiting for us to simply pick them up and use them. The practice of engaging with our dreamed Nightmares teaches us how to do so in waking life. Resolving Nightmares helps us resolve problems in our waking life.

When we deny the importance of the inner messages of our dreams, and the clear effect they have on our bodies, we are denying the voice of our inner self. This creates inner confusion. Saying that a Nightmare is meaningless, for example, when our physical bodies are still shaken by it, is a lie. It's like sweating profusely in full summer sun and telling ourselves we're not hot. Denying these clear physical messages over time leads us to question whether or not we can trust our gut or listen to our inner voice, or even know how to find it. Then we feel quite separate from our intuiting inner self. Acknowledging the messages of our dreams is a first step to repairing this inner trust.

Repetitive Nightmares

Nightmares work *for* us. When we refuse to pay attention to them, they continue their efforts by repeating. In fact, they double down. This is the second kind of dream, the Repetitive Nightmare. Repetitive Nightmares are the exact same scene, the exact same Nightmare, that plays over and over and over. And over—even over a period of years.

We can think of this Repetitive Nightmare as a friend whose call you ignore. Likely this friend will send a text, ping you on social media, and then even call, trying every way to get their message to you. Eventually this friend may arrive at your door, pounding loudly to try to get you to open up and see the emergency just outside. This is what the Repetitive Nightmare is trying to do—alert you to a problem. Problems don't go away until and unless we face them, and Repetitive Nightmares signal that we are disregarding something that we need to address.

In one example of a Repetitive Nightmare a woman dreams that a terrifying man is knocking at her door. In each dream, just as she arrives at the door she wakes up in a fright. This dream appeared night after night until she figured out a way to resolve it.

The scenario of a Repetitive Nightmare is quite specific: a situation occurs and moves forward just to the stuck moment. The movement to the stuck moment—which, in the dream, is when we wake up—is a fixed pattern. Like a needle caught in a record groove, the pattern plays to the stuck image, only to skip back and start again, over and over, until the dreamer finally gets tired of the repetition and moves the needle. As soon as this happens, the Repetitive Nightmare resolves, shifting both the image and the waking perspective, and forward motion resumes.

For the woman with the terrifying man knocking at her door, the Repetitive Nightmare resolved as soon as she opened the door. The man turned out to be a loving aspect of the Self. She never had the terrifying dream again.

Busy Dreams

The third kind of dream is the Busy Dream. These dreams are known for their diffuse colors and details. They are brown, hazy or dusty, mottled, unclear, or murky. They usually contain a lot of people, with a lot of things going on, none of which is particularly interesting, and none of which is fully formed or coheres into a complete story. Busy Dreams never engage the dreamer viscerally; instead, they leave the same physical impression as the unclear, unformed atmosphere of them. They feel as if they go on forever, lasting all night, moving from one disconnected vignette to another, after which you wake up feeling as if you've never fully slept. Busy Dreams are tiring to experience, and they leave us tired upon waking.

Busy Dreams come from the anxieties and worries, agitations and stresses that have built up around an issue that is not being faced. For this reason, Busy Dreams frequently follow on the heels of an ignored Nightmare and an ignored Repetitive Nightmare. If we don't listen to the Nightmare, it repeats to get our attention; if we still don't listen, then what was originally a simple scenario with a simple resolve gets complicated.

Think of Busy Dreams as originating in this way: There is an initial problem, let's say, a fight with a friend for missing a planned meetup. This is immediate, obvious, and might be signaled by a Nightmare. At this stage we can easily address it. If we ignore it, though, the Nightmare may repeat.

Ignoring both the Nightmare and the Repetitive Nightmare has consequences. Secondary emotions and additional conflicts arise in reaction to the original issue. If you don't address the problem of the missed meetup, for example, you might begin to feel a vague and general sense of distance from your friend and a growing lack of trust. This might lead to lack of communication altogether. Lack of communication stirs a new set of emotions, from anger to abandonment, fear, neediness, or sadness. These secondary emotions eventually begin to take over when you think about this friend. As a result, you lose the thread of the real issue, the first simple missed meeting. All the secondary, murky, unclear emotions and perceptions that creep in when we don't deal with the Nightmare are the material of a Busy Dream.

The Busy Dream is a pile-up of all the undealt-with emotions and additional conflicts spurred by the original issue. The agitations, restless movements from here to there, and tiring sensations of the Busy Dream derive from ongoing daytime nervous emotions that lack clarification and distinction. Because we've lost the thread of the original issue over time, we feel a vague unsettled sense but don't locate it. That vagueness is mirrored in the vague scenarios and sienna colors of the Busy Dream. Busy Dreams indicate that the dreamer's inner world is busied by emotional reactions and distractions that keep the dreamer from facing their real issue.

Unresolved problems beget more problems. Think of a house. If I leave a pair of socks on the living room floor, I won't need to make much of an effort to clean it up. If day after day after day, however, I leave more socks on the floor, I create a pile. Then I start to stress over the pile (not the socks!) because it seems like too much to try and tackle. Maybe I throw a blanket over it to try to hide it, but then I have an even bigger mess to clean up. Where do I start? Plus, the first pair of socks were white—I know what load and laundry cycle to put them in. But now there are whites and darks and reds and brights. How do I sort them? Which do I attend to first? The simple problem of a pair of socks on the floor is now compounded by the problem of not dealing with the problem, begetting myriad other problems.

We frequently do "piling up" in our daily lives. Once a client told me on our first meeting that he was about to get fired and needed help getting a new job. "Nothing works here anymore," he said. "Nothing works here anymore" is a vague and murky sentence which signaled to me that this was a waking time Busy Dream. Remember in the last chapter we looked at how language can give us a hint about what inner images we are experiencing? Without even starting to work with this client's night dreams, I knew what he was dreaming because of the vague, obtuse, anxiety-colored way he spoke about his situation. So, I worked with him in waking time exactly as if I was working with a Busy Dream—sorting through the pile.

Soon the scenario became clear: a new manager had recently replaced the previous manager of fifteen years. This new manager shifted each team member's role, and my client was suddenly doing something completely new after a decade and a half of comfortable competence. The new manager had given frequent feedback that my client took as increasingly negative. The original issue was merely that the client needed to learn a new skill set and computer program, but my client reacted in fear. This initial moment was a Nightmare. He didn't address this fear, however, and his inner situation quickly spiraled to include many secondary emotions expressed as his anxiety over aging, worry about not having an adequate retirement package, and—finally—a firm belief he was about to be fired. Rather than simply learn a new computer program, his numerous emotional reactions led him to obsess over his LinkedIn profile, CV, and how to find a new job.

The gift of the Busy Dream is that it helps us recognize when we are piling up. Once clued in, we can dig past the symptoms to identify the core cause. When we get to the original problem and finally face it, all the secondary emotions and issues will naturally dissipate or, now manageable, be easily sorted out.

Clear Dreams

Quite different from the three kinds of dreams discussed so far is the fourth, the Clear Dream. Clear Dreams are characterized by a coherent, clear story line. We can recount Clear Dreams to someone in a way that feels like we're telling a story with distinct details, characters, and even a sense of a beginning, middle, and end. Sometimes the dream has exposition and backstory ("*I knew already in the dream that James had been to a party and was coming to meet me*"), a through-line ("*First, we're in the house. . . later we're in the car*"), and perhaps even an action or character arc. Their colors are everyday colors. Often, they will be punctuated by a particular color that stands out—a bright red sweater, a yellow pair of shoes, a blue tent. Sometimes this particular color repeats in different forms, as a leitmotif; a carton of creamy white milk shows up later as a white Bentley car, for example.

All dreams show us where we are in the present, and what is possible in the future. Nightmares, Repetitive Nightmares, and Busy Dreams are implicit in their possibility—by showing us what is wrong, we know that facing the challenge to respond to them will unlock a potential that has been held back. The Clear Dream, however, is uniquely explicit in revealing where we are, where we can be, what is blocking us from getting there, and how to surmount that block.

Clear Dreams will very often show us energies we've ignored, hidden talents, and latent abilities we've overlooked or disregarded. By revealing these beneficial aspects, Clear Dreams bring us far beyond the more critical, situational address of the Nightmare and into the realm of *self-becoming*.

It's like the difference between putting out a fire (Nightmare) and developing a strategic plan (Clear Dream). Clear Dreams offer more refined angles, different perspectives, and nuance. Theirs is often a scenario where new rooms or cities appear ready to be explored, with discoveries to be made. All these discoveries are forgotten capabilities that are now brought forward to be remembered.

Clear Dreams become more frequent as we clear up the Nightmares of our lives. Once we get the urgent emotional alarms of Nightmares taken care of and sort through the secondary emotions of our piling-on tendencies, we arrive at a place where we can finally start to grow. We can think of this as clearing a field in order to plant a garden: first we have to remove all the rocks, then we have to break the hard crust of ground to get to the fertile soil below. Once there, we can plant seeds, as well as discover existing shoots that were waiting for open space to emerge.

Like Nightmares, Repetitive Nightmares, and Busy Dreams, Clear Dreams can also be found by looking at our waking life experiences. We find them often when it's time to make a choice, which involves bringing forward a pushed-aside aspect of the Self. Clear Dreams also appear when we can stretch and do more in some area of our inner evolution.

One example of a Clear Dream appearing in waking life is that of a recent client who had a very good job, a happy family life, and was financially stable. This person literally had nothing to complain about. . . except the inner experience was getting mundane. Days were humdrum rather than exciting. A little talking revealed that there was, in fact, a next step: a career that was in line with their current field of work, but that would require leaving a company position to assume a more entrepreneurial role. The prospect of a new opportunity was enticing but was mentioned in an "I'll get there at some point" kind of way. Why? Because despite this person's expertise in the field, the shift from in-house to self-employed was a big jump, and contentment in life was turning into complacency. Looked at through the lens of a Clear Dream, this person saw the block of complacency clearly, and the desire to make the jump—now, not at some point—became obvious.

From Night to Day and Back to Night

I wrote in an earlier chapter that what we are dreaming at night we are living in the day. By now you realize this is not a one-to-one correspondence; dreams at night (and our inner images during the day) include other information, like what we are not living but would like to be and inner potentials we have pushed aside, judged, or left dormant.

Because dreams are in response to our waking life experiences, understanding the seven kinds of dreams will not only help you better understand your night dreams, it will give you insights into your waking experience. Using these kinds of dreams as a lens to view your waking time is like sewing together the parts of ourselves that we see clearly alongside the parts that dreams help us see. This turbocharges our inner growth and self-awareness and makes our ability to see and correct errors quick and responsive.

For example, if you dream a Nightmare at night, that means that there is an element of Nightmare in some aspect of your current waking life. In waking life, we may not have taken the time to reflect upon what we are experiencing, purposely ignored this Nightmare element, or not recognized it because we're driven by patterns and habits. The Nightmare signals us to inspect our waking time to identify and respond to the element of Nightmare lurking there. The same is true of each of the seven kinds of dreams, which help us move from dream to waking and back again.

We can also do the reverse and move from waking to dream. You can do this by first discerning what kind of dream you would use to characterize a waking life experience. For example, an uncomfortable situation at work may feel like a Nightmare in the moment but may not, in fact, have been an actual Nightmare when you look at it through the rubric of the seven kinds of dreams. Instead, you may find it to be a Clear Dream that gives you a clear message. Making this distinction opens us to finding what, specifically, needs to be addressed in the interaction and how to respond to it. Working with a life experience in the same way we work with a dream experience gives us a well-defined road map of how we can understand and stay responsive in situations and relationships.

Our life experience is seamless, like a long, continually unrolling scroll. Because life is in constant motion, it can be difficult to see how events are connected, notice patterns, or make sense of decisions and their consequences. Looking at waking life experiences as a kind of dream puts little pauses in this flow. This helps us to sort through these moving sensations and events and to break them into discrete, comprehensible chapters.

Also, because life experience is always unrolling, there can be a lengthy lag time between what we experience in the present tense, what we come to understand about that experience, and how we feel about it. How often do we think, "I wish I had thought to reply this way. . . " or "If only I had done X, Y, Z. . . " Our response to experiences is often far removed from the moment it happened. In that lag time, we can make many decisions and errors. It's like stepping into a dark room and yet continuing to walk forward without waiting to register that it's dark or looking for a flashlight.

Working with dreams shortens the gap between experience and response. First, our night dreams clue us in to what is happening in our waking time. This instills a more conscious inspection of our day, which in return gives us insights into what kind of "dream" we are living. This moves us closer to living in the present where we can begin to consciously direct our life rather than "playing catch up" and trying to correct previous errors.

What Dream Are You Dreaming? Distinguishing Between Dreams

So far, we've explored four kinds of dreams: Nightmares, Repetitive Nightmares, Busy Dreams, and Clear Dreams. How easy is it to make distinctions between them? The following excerpt is from a dream that a client presented in a class as a Nightmare. But is it? As you read it, see if you can determine what kind of dream it is.

> *I'm in a dance workshop. The teacher shows a complex series of moves one time, and then we have to dance it full out. I'm with my friend who has the same name as me. The teacher is pushy, going too fast. I can't find the time I need to make the moves precise. My friend doesn't have a problem, but I am not able to do the moves. My hair was in a bun, but now it's loose and messy. I decide to go slower to be more precise in my movements, but then I lose my friend.*
>
> *It's Saturday, and I want to go to the beach with another friend. The city is narrow; I want to get out. We go to the coast—it's beautiful! There is a traffic jam coming back to the city in the evening.*
>
> *Now I'm in a city with a river running through it. I'm going to swim with another friend. There is a floating ring, but she takes it before I can try it out myself. I jump in anyway, and we have fun.*
>
> *I want to sit and study, but the news says there has been an explosion in the city, including the library that I like to go to. The library's beautiful colored-glass front is destroyed. I want to meet three friends, but the nice café has been destroyed, so someone suggests we go to a bar. Inside, it is dark. There is an old, large swimming pool, which is empty. I sit on a couch by the pool and the fabric starts to move—it turns into hands and legs. A man in a black mask is grabbing me! I scream, but everyone is frozen.*

The dream undoubtedly contains nightmarish elements. The final scene of the couch-turned-man grabbing at the dreamer is terrifying, and it woke the original dreamer with all the body signals of Nightmare: pounding heart, sweating, and a sense of fear. Some of the other elements in the dream, however, suggest something quite different.

At the heart of the dream is a river that flows. The dreamer jumps into it and has fun. In another moment, the dreamer goes to the coast and it's beautiful. The felt sense of fun, flowing, and beautiful are not Nightmare elements. So, what, exactly, is the dream?

Let's step into the dream as if I'm the dreamer. The dream begins with a challenge. I'm in a new situation that feels fast and pushes me. One part of me (the girl with the same name) keeps up with the challenge, while another part of me (the "me" in the dream) feels overwhelmed and disheveled by it (hair loose and messy). That disheveled "me" steps out of the dance, which is to say steps out of the challenge altogether. I lose the part of myself that can keep up. Stepping out from a challenge is the beginning of the problem. Eventually it is going to lead to the frozen sensation that concludes the dream, from stepping out to completely stopped motion.

The next scene shows us again, in a different way, what is happening in the body: the city (which also represents an aspect of the "me" of the dream) feels narrow. The dreamer wants out of this narrow sensation and finds a way out by going to a coast, which provides an expanded view (coastal horizon). The expanded coast is aligned with the dancer with my name who can keep up with the moves in the first part of the dream. Returning to the narrow city, and the traffic jam, is the "me" dancer that stepped out of the challenge and is disheveled. This, too, is mirrored in the frozen sensation that concludes the dream. Stepping out of challenge leads to stopped traffic, which leads to the frozen, or stopped, movement at the end of the dream. Stuck.

The situation is evident: at exactly the same time the dreamer has one aspect of the Self which is capable, able to keep up with the present challenge and able to maintain an expanded view of things, while another aspect of the Self feels overwhelmed and pushed by the challenge, disheveled, narrowed, and finally jammed, stepping out of engaging with the challenge altogether. The stuck aspect is later mirrored in the bar (read the pun!), with the people (the dreamer's energies) being frozen and unable to come to aid.

The waking life moment when the dreamer had this dream was during the initial lockdowns of the COVID-19 virus in 2020. This emotional challenge leaves her disheveled and, eventually, stuck. The place she enjoys going, the library in the dream, is her inner emotional space, which has been damaged by the explosion she heard about on the news. The café is likewise destroyed and replaced by a dark bar. The dreamer sinks into a place of fear, the *masked* fear, that threatens to pull her in and not let her move.

The dream ends in a stuck place. Dreams, however, are holistic and therefore are all-time or all-at-once. Like a painting with many elements, though we look at and describe each element in turn, it remains one single image. Even though linear time orders us to speak of one part of a dream before another, all parts are simultaneously present. The part of us that is capable in this dream, in other words, is as right-now as the stuck part of us.

Notice the contrasts in this dream between the capable dancer and the disheveled one who steps out, the flowing river and the empty pool, the narrow city/jammed traffic and the expanded coast, and the jumping in versus sitting out. The aspects that are disheveled, stepping out, jammed, and frozen are the "me" of the dreamer, which is to say the perspective the dreamer is holding in waking life. (We'll talk more about the waking perspective that we bring into our dreams in a later chapter.) The latent aspects of "me" in the dream are the dancer with the "same name as me" who knows the steps, the expanded coast, fun, jumping in, and flow. These latent aspects are existing perspectives and abilities that the dreamer is not seeing in waking life, but which are revealing themselves in the dream. We can think of these as the higher or dreaming self. The dream may end in being stuck, in our linear reading of it, but the holistic aspect of the dream shows that the expanded and capable self is also present and equally, immediately accessible.

A clear storyline, everyday colors with one more brightly colored aspect (the stained-glass window), and a sense of beginning, middle, and end—this dream is a Clear Dream. Did you guess it?

Notice how this Clear Dream goes beyond simply showing a conflict; it also reveals capable aspects of the dreamer that she can activate in waking life. As a Clear Dream it shows where the dreamer currently is (frozen in the face of the shocking new challenge) and where the dreamer can be (flowing and having fun). We see quite plainly what is blocking the dreamer from getting there: the fear she showed in the dance class, when she slowed down to perfect the dance. It's the same part of her that is seeking a security float when the friend jumps in the water. And we see in the dream how to surmount that block: jump in anyway. The result, after all, is "we have fun."

Events and challenges in life happen. Whether we react to them or respond to them, whether we suffer them or maintain equilibrium, is our choice. Clear Dreams present choice along with showing us the tools we have for making the change from a waking, limited perspective, to the expanded dreaming one.

In our dream example, all aspects of the Self were previously integrated. We see that in the colorful window of perspective that interfaced between the interior of the library—containing all that the dreamer knows about joy, dancing, and flow (what the teacher was showing in the initial steps of the dance)—and the outside world. The explosion of the changed life situation with COVID-19 exploded that colorful window, separating these two aspects; pulling apart the dancer who knows the steps and the one who steps out. Reintegrating, which the dreaming self already knows how to do, is the key.

Nightmares show us energies that are completely tied up, but Clear Dreams provide multiple perspectives. The choice this Clear Dream presents is between returning to the place of flow that is already present or allowing oneself to sink into and be captured by fear. Returning to flow is something already experienced in the dream. The part of the dreamer that can jump into change and have fun with it is as present as the part that is frozen. Therefore, the dreamer can choose which aspect she wishes to move from, now, in her waking life.

Great Dreams, Light Dreams, and Dreams of Union

Nightmare, the Repetitive Nightmare, the Busy Dream, and the Clear Dream are characterized by specific colors: dark, mottled or diffuse, or everyday colors. They contain specific emotions or feelings, such as fear, anger, frustration, or the thrill of a discovery. They also have notable visceral details, such as going too fast, freezing, stepping out, jumping in, or heart pounding. The colors and physical experiences of these dreams are familiar to us, because we experience them at different times in our waking lives, even sometimes all within one day. They characterize our common, quotidian interactions, like a score playing in the background of our waking life that leads our steps forward or stops us in our tracks.

The next three kinds of dreams—Great Dreams, Light Dreams, and Dreams of Union—belong to another set of physical and sensorial experiences that are also part of human life and yet belong to another element of existence: the place of awe, and the extraordinary. Like holding a newborn, looking into the vast sky and seeing the Milky Way, or our sense of love transcendent, these expansive experiences bring us in touch with that which lies beyond us, the wonder and marvel of the mystery of life. These, too, are lived experiences, which means that these, too, are dreams.

The Great Dream

The Great Dream is short. It is characterized by exceedingly brilliant, jewel-like colors, beyond what we see and know in waking time. They often have vivid sensations beyond the visual—smells, tastes, music or sounds, synesthesia, tactile sensations, and sensations of expansion or other visceral details. Beethoven was said to have composed music for instruments that had not yet been invented, but which he heard in his dreams. Great Dreams have—or are—a message. This is often understood by the dreamer as a deep, inner knowing that may or may not be able to be verbally expressed.

An example of a Great Dream is this:

> *I am flying across the ocean, very fast. It is night. It is so beautiful. In front of me, on the horizon, are giant images, like supernovas, in the shape of giant lions like you see on European coats of arms or the symbol of Peugeot. Plumes of color—greens, violets, purples, deep blues—all the bright colors of the cosmos.*

The colors of this dream are the saturated, vivid brilliant colors of a Great Dream, the dream is short, and in this case, there is a message. The dream is mine, and the message was immediately and completely clear to me. The clarity of inner knowing elicited in the dream, and the intense, expansive, awe-inspiring experience of it, confirmed a choice I had made to make a great life change. We will look at dreams like this again and explore how to respond to their messages in Chapter Ten.

Not every Great Dream will have an overt message. Experiencing wonder and marvel, in all the parts of our being, is a gift of the Great Dream and message enough; we, and life, are never the same after. Such experiences remind us that there is more to life than tackling a to-do list, paying bills, work, and errands. Beyond these quotidian aspects of our existence are those of inspiration, creativity, and revelation. Integrating our everyday, linear life with the revelatory experiences that cause us to reach higher is key to being a whole person. Living the experience of our Great Dream is our response to it.

Light Dreams and Dreams of Union

Beyond message and particularity are Light Dreams. Light Dreams are simply that—dream experiences of light, in whatever color or colors they're experienced. There are no objects, characters, or thoughts—just the experience of light.

Similarly, Dreams of Union are the experience of unity and oneness. In these dreams there is no form, no ego, no sense of "I." They are—simply and profoundly—a return to the experience of "all one."

The Fluid Ladder of Dreaming

While it may feel as if there is a hierarchy to the seven kinds of dreams, or that one naturally leads to the other in neat steps, that is not exactly the case. Different kinds of dreams are not moved through in a static or linear way. We may have a Nightmare one night and, if we've resolved it, have a Clear Dream another night. . . only to return to a Nightmare later that very week when facing a new challenge. Just as our living experiences are a journey through various terrains, so, too, is our dreaming response. No attainment of a higher state remains fixed. Life is ever moving, we are ever evolving, and our dreams are part of, and present to, that dynamic experience.

We have to be careful not to be tricked into imposing a value system on dreams or to say, for example, that Great Dreams are "better" than Nightmares. It is true that facing our Nightmares and resolving them clears us to be a receiving vessel for the Great Dreams of our lives. However, the signals of Nightmares telling us that we've fallen out of balance are just as integral to our inner growth as is a Great Dream. Likewise, to get over blocks, we need Clear Dreams to recognize them, and to shine a light on other perspectives and abilities we possess so that we can respond and move into possibility.

We have to be careful, too, of the tendency to characterize a present waking experience as one kind of dream and then expect to dream accordingly. For example, I have had clients say, "Life is great right now, why am I not having Great Dreams?" Dreams *do* reflect our present-tense experiencing, but we are often not fully aware of this present-tense experiencing. Our waking view of things is a thin slice that dreams seek to fill out, like a using a mirror to see the back of our head.

The clients who ask why they aren't having Great Dreams when life seems "great" are often experiencing the comfort of familiar pattern, calling that comfort "great right now." However, comfort, familiarity, or lack of overt conflict is not necessarily "great." Dreams are always going to challenge us to continue evolving. Perhaps there is another layer to peel back, or another possibility waiting for us. Dreams are both in step with us and ahead of us, showing us things we skip over, race past, don't see, or ignore in our own inner self or in the outer world. "Great right now" isn't necessarily "the best of me." Dreaming knows if more is possible.

The very fact of putting expectation onto dream *is* a blockage. Being a true dreamer is learning to receive without expectation, assumption, or values, and being open to whatever the dream chooses to reveal—the habit that needs correction, the familiar that needs shaking, or the marvelous that needs seeing.

In the next chapter we'll look a little closer at these kinds of dreams and see how we can sort them into two different categories.

CHAPTER FOUR

Recognizing the Resolved and Unresolved in Dreams

"I dream that my friend John tells me that he and his husband divorced because he had to finish fixing his house back home. I tell him I was just talking about that —a friend and I are looking to buy a house that needs to be renovated. I told him: 'No house can be left unfinished.'"

—Dreamer

A frightened woman on one side of a closed door as someone tries to get in, a car careening out of control toward a gaping hole, a dancer losing her steps and eventually falling into a couch-man's grasp, a golden almond with a box blocking the path to it. We encountered these dreams over the last few chapters. In each of them there is a sense of something not quite finished, like a film ending right in the middle of the conflict, an intergalactic battle cut off before we know who wins.

By contrast, we've also seen a dream of vivid, brilliant colors, flying across an ocean, a supernova-like sight in the heavens that engendered a clear inner knowing in the dreamer. This dream is the whole story. One unbroken experience. This dream feels resolved, closed, complete.

We discovered in the last chapter that there are seven different kinds of dreams, but we can sort these seven into two broad categories: resolved or unresolved. This chapter takes a look at these two categories, including how to identify them and how to use them to interact with both your night dreams and waking life as tools for transformation.

Unresolved Dreams

The body-being's natural state is balance. Whenever we are thrown off balance, the body seeks to resolve the issue and return to a state of balance. In scientific terms, this is called homeostasis and the classic example of this is body temperature. If the body temperature begins to drop, for example, we start to shiver, the hair stands up on our arms and legs, and other physical mechanisms engage to help raise it. Likewise, when we are too hot, our body begins to sweat to increase heat evaporation and cool us off.

Balance, or homeostasis, includes more than just our physical body. We can think of ourselves as having four aspects of a body-being: physical, emotional, mental, and spiritual. Each one of these four aspects seeks to be in balance. When they are balanced, we can think of them as vibrating harmonically, each supporting the other. Off-balance, they engage mechanisms to alert us to restore them to harmony.

Nightmares are one such mechanism. The acute message of the Nightmare is that the harmonious vibration of balance has been disrupted. Depicting that disruption via the emotions and images of the Nightmare engages our conscious attention. We, then, as conscious attenders, are responsible for rebalancing ourselves. Either we interact directly with the content of the dream, or we make changes in our waking life to address the problem.

Like Nightmares, Repetitive Nightmares, Busy Dreams, and Clear Dreams also alert us to an aspect of the self that is off-balance and needs to return to balance. Each of these dreams contains something to either repair or bring forward from dormancy to action. These dreams belong to the category of Unresolved Dreams.

Recognizing the Unresolved

The entire content of dreams—the images, forms, emotions, colors, sounds, narratives, and other phenomenon—are tangible manifestations of our body-energy. If that energy is tangled or blocked, suppressed or overcharged in some way, then we'll have an Unresolved Dream.

In the four aspects of our body-being—physical, emotional, mental, and spiritual —an imbalance in one sets off an imbalance in all the others. We can illustrate this with the experience of hunger. At first hunger is merely physical. If not heeded, a person becomes irritable or angry (emotional), their ability to concentrate rapidly diminishes (mental), and with all these alarms going off, there is no energy left for tending to higher matters, like creating a loving or soulful experience (spiritual).

Imbalance is easy to identify because it is an embodied experience that we recognize, just like we do balance. To walk, we wobble a bit as we lift a foot to step forward, then regain footing and balance as we set it down. Similarly, we first feel fatigue, then restfulness once we sleep. This understanding of temporary imbalance, followed by an urge to right it, is an integral part of our physical being-ness. Like walking, life cycles also begin in a place of balance, then get opened out in the process of change—which is destabilizing—and then brought back into balance; from resting state to action we then look to completion, which is a return to resting state.

As humans, we naturally seek resolution, the exhale that brings us back to center. We crave resolution in narratives. We seek narrative structure whether we're reading verbal or visual stories, or hearing verbal narratives and sentence structures.[1] When a friend dangles off in telling us a story, we demand *So how did it end?* We even hear it in movements of a symphony with a minor key leaving us with a sense of the unfinished, seeking a return to a major key to "complete" the piece.[2] In a romance, lovers torn apart by circumstance makes us yearn for the change that will reunite them. We wait for the period at the end of the sentence.

In dreaming, as in waking life, out of control cars want to be controlled, calls that can't connect want to go through, planes circling endlessly in the sky seek to land. This chapter opens with a dream in which there is a house that needs to be "finished." And, as the dreamer said in the dream, "*No house can be left unfinished.*" In our body-being, nothing wants to be left unfinished, either.

Recognizing that something isn't complete, that things remain unresolved, is the first step of responding to an imbalance in our system. After that, we have to know what needs to be done to rebalance it. Does an endlessly circling plane need to land, or does it need to be directed to a new destination? In a house that still needs to be finished what, specifically, do we do next?

The aspect of the dream that needs our active involvement to complete is called the **Necessity** of the dream. All Unresolved Dreams contain a Necessity. The Necessity is the pivot point that will shift imbalance to balance. In our dreaming dialogue, we bring things back to balance by responding to the Necessity. When we do, it redirects the energies of the body—all of them—back to harmonious vibration. Just as one aspect of our body-being sliding off-balance tips the others out of balance, addressing the one Necessity brings all of them back into balance.

The house that still needs "finishing" illustrates how important addressing a Necessity is. The dream speaks of a relationship that ends in a divorce because of this undone aspect. It is not only our relationship with self that is resolved when addressing a Necessity; our relationships with others, too, are affected. Whatever our inner experience is directly corresponds to our outer, waking world. An inner issue left in a state of "unfinished fixing" means our outer relationships are equally suspended or disrupted. Both need us to address the Necessities of our dreams—"finish fixing the house"—to bring back to union any unresolved issues with others.

The Necessity is the linchpin of change. It is the element on which our inner development hangs. Let's take a more detailed look at how to identify it in both dreaming and waking time.

Necessities and the Shift from Unresolved to Resolved

All of the four Unresolved Dreams have an area of conflict or place of imbalance. Because of this, we can say that these dreams remain open, or in need of further work, with the ultimate work being to resolve the conflict. Between the conflict and resolve is what we call the Necessity. The Necessity is *the* action that will move the dream from conflict to resolve, open to closed. A dream may contain numerous areas that indicate conflict and imbalance, but there will only be one Necessity.

Like a magic key, finding the Necessity and turning it in the lock of conflict unlocks all the other areas that were off-balance. Think back to our example of being hungry. While physical hunger knocked the emotional, mental, and spiritual aspects of the body-being off-balance, at the bottom of the issue is needing to eat. The inability to concentrate will be resolved by eating, we'll regain the ability to manage our hunger-driven emotions and make amends to those whom we've lashed out at, and instead of having to deal with the physical alarm of the basic need of hunger, our life-flow energy will be available to attend to our spiritual self, which will be returned to our naturally harmonious and creative state. Many things were off-balance, but all are brought back into place by identifying and addressing the one Necessity: eating.

Hunger is a waking-time example. Let's see how this plays out in a dream Nightmare. Here is a dream we looked at in Chapter Three: the Nightmare of the car about to crash.

> *I'm in a car that's going way too fast. It's dark, we can barely see the road. So many people are crammed in the car, and the music is turned up so loud. Suddenly I see there's a giant, gaping hole in the road up ahead. There's no way we can stop in time—we're going to fall in!*

The dream is clearly unresolved—it's heading for a crash. Without this dramatic trajectory, however, there are numerous aspects of this dream that signal imbalance in the body-being of the dreamer. Let's start with the word "too." The car is going *too* fast. I see this also in the use of "so," as in *so* many people with the music turned up *so* loud. It's also "too dark"; though that "too" is left out of explicit verbalization, we understand it by "barely able to see the road." "Too" and "so" here are both expressing something that is over a normal amount. Too fast, too dark, too many people, and too loud—none of these are the body's experience of balance. Balance is never "over"—it is always "just right."

The word "too" in dream descriptions is one signal of off-balance. You may notice a too-loud crowd, a too-windy or too-dry desert terrain. Maybe it appears as too many characters running around without aim. Or perhaps it shows as not enough of something, like not enough light to see, which is showing that it's too dark. "Too" is not a word we associate with serenity, peace, or awe; neither is lack. If "too much" of something or "not enough" of another appears in a dream, this is an easy flag of a place to start looking at more closely to identify an imbalance and its Necessity—both in dream and waking life.

Notice that after this slew of expressions of something that is "too" much for the dreamer, the next image is a giant gaping hole. Remember that dreams are showing us in image and context the current state of our body-energies and reflecting back our present waking reality. The pattern of imbalance shown in this dream is about to terminate in falling into a hole—in dream and waking time. The energies of this dreamer, off-centered in "too-much," are about to crash. The imbalance of "too" cannot be maintained—total stop is the body's inevitable resolve to restore balance unless the dreamer heeds the message and consciously intervenes in waking life to wrest their energies back to equilibrium.

Modern life is, in many ways, characterized by "too." We work too much, sleep too little, have too little time. Here's an exercise to see this for yourself: For one week listen to how you describe scenarios and events in your day and see if you can catch when and how something appears as "too." When you see it, identify the exact imbalance—is it too much work, too much indulgence? If so, in what way, specifically? Be as specific as possible to get to the exact origin of it. Then, follow it to see how this experience of "too" has led to other imbalances, like lashing out when irritably hungry. Finally, say out loud in a sentence the imbalance and the Necessity, and ask yourself what needs to be done right now to respond to it. For example: hunger, need to eat, eat. Then do it. If it's to eat, then really sit down and eat. What changes when you do? Once you've responded to the Necessity, you may then want to put back in order any disturbances the imbalance had caused, such as apologizing to someone if you did lash out while in that state.

Because you are now well into your dream practice, you can also look to see where your dreams are showing "too." During the same week of the exercise, each morning highlight or underline all the appearances of "too" that you find in your dreams. Then, read out loud just the words or phrases you have highlighted. What do you learn by hearing it? Are you able to trace the lines between that and the use of "too" in your waking time?

In the "too" Nightmare of the car heading for a crash, the Necessity was to stop the car. In waking life this dreamer was on a long, grueling work trip with too many meetings, too little sleep and time, racing from presentation to airport and back to presentation, eating too little or too much, and being gone too long from home. Had I not heard the night dream I would have still "heard the dream" in the waking client session, not only with the excesses and shortcomings, but also within their racing, breathless description of what was going on. Notice the energetic tempo of this racing and breathless description and how it mirrors the fast, loud, "racing toward the hole" description of, and movements in, the dream. Paying attention to what we are dreaming shows us what we are living. As we've been discussing, waking and dreaming life are reflected in each other.

When we begin to notice imbalances, find their Necessity, and resolve them, we free our energies to use them in creative efforts, rather than remaining blocked and preoccupied with unaddressed needs. Imagine walking around all day if your night dream has shown that you are racing toward a gaping hole. This means that while you are giving a presentation, for example, or having a discussion with your boss, in your body—what you think of as in the back of your mind—there are massive alarms sounding an SOS that a gaping hole is right up ahead! What do you think the quality of your presentation or discussion will be as result? Or imagine having a Nightmare of an overflowing toilet at night, and the next day hosting a dinner party with friends. In the "house of Self" there is an overflowing toilet. If you imagine that as the house where the dinner party is taking place, how relaxed will you be in conversation knowing that "down the hall" is an overflowing toilet?

The imbalances signaled by our night dreams don't disappear upon waking—they continue to play out in our daily waking experience. We may attempt to shove them to our peripheries, but they remain front and center regardless. They show up as an inability to be present; as irritations, frustrations, and other emotions that underline interactions; as ongoing conflicts with others; as the "tapes" that play over and over in the mind; and as being drained of energy, lacking passion, or feeling uncreative.

The very practical aspect of dreaming is that we can find these imbalances in our night dreams and deal with them. We can also learn to hear our waking time descriptions of what we are experiencing as a dream and identify imbalances there. This small shift of perception is a powerful tool for becoming intensely present and for having agency in your life.

With the dreamer of the car about to crash, I did a waking dream exercise. You've already been introduced to this exercise in Chapter Two with the woman who saw the box on the path between her and the golden almond. In this case, I had the dreamer close her eyes, see and feel that she returns to the dream, and step into the car consciously to bring it to a stop. As soon as the dreamer consciously takes the wheel, the "too loud" music is quiet, the sun comes out, and the driver is alone in the car in relieved, silent calm.

The calm changed everything in the dreamer's body-energy. Now the dreamer could think clearly. The impending disaster was obvious, as was the need to avert it. So, in addition to this exercise, she responded in waking life by telling her office that the remainder of the trip needed to be rescheduled so she could return home to regroup. Having done this, the dreamer avoided crashing in waking time too. The question is: If the dreamer was so pained in waking life, telling me that things were "too much," why had the dreamer not rescheduled the rest of the trip already?

When unbalanced, it is difficult to see how to find a solution; our creative energies are bound up in the imbalance. It is as if the entire creative department of a company is sent to work triage in a hospital, leaving the company's creative offices empty and gathering dust. A body imbalance is a body emergency, and all energies are asked to be on hand to deal with it.

While we're at it, we can ask ourselves why we don't stop and eat when we are hungry, or sleep if we are tired. Life moves very quickly and presents us with a lot of seeming urgencies. When alarm bells are ringing in our body, signaling that we are off-balance, it is difficult to pause long enough to identify what, exactly, is ringing the alarm. Instead, we react to the urgency of the *alarm*, rather than the urgency of the *Necessity*. We drink coffee when tired and "slog through it" or eat a candy bar and "tough it out." Neither of these are real fixes, however, and will eventually move from a Nightmare waking (and dreaming) situation to a Repetitive Nightmare, or worse.

It is equally difficult to sort through which alarm to pay attention to if multiple alarms are happening at the same time. With the example of hunger, the body is hungry, but our partner may also have hurt feelings from the irritable text we shot their way when we were hungry. On top of that, we may have a looming work deadline that caused us to put off eating in the first place. Still, with these alarms, the Necessity remains the same: to eat. Trying to salve a bad communication with a partner while still irritable doesn't work. Neither does trying to deal with a deadline. Research on students who miss even one meal has shown a drop in concentration and a tendency to make errors in even routine tasks.[3] On top of the emotional disturbance of irritability, you have a ripe stew for accidentally sending a complaining email to a co-worker.

Paying attention to your dreams will help you to quickly recognize when you've fallen out of balance. Identifying the Necessities will help you come back. Applying this to your waking life, you'll bring the two sides of your doing and experiencing-knowing self into alignment and into the present. This means that problems that could compound due to inattention and festering are resolved while they are still simple.

Imbalances show up in dreams in many ways. We looked at "too," which is a common and easily identifiable one. Another easy place to start is where things "just don't feel right" in dreams. Maybe it's a mood, a color, a misplaced object like the cardboard box between the dreamer and the golden almond. Imbalance shows up in jerky movements and incomplete actions such as missing a train, not being able to get a call to go through, or not being able to find a phone or wallet. We find imbalance in colors and physical sensations that are displeasing; a recent client had the color yellow in her dream, of which she said: "I don't like [it]. I don't know why, but it feels dull or lifeless, muted." If in doubt, return to sensation. Ask yourself, does "lifeless yellow" feel balanced? Does having a "box between me and a golden almond" feel resolved in the body? Whatever the scenario of the dream, your body will tell you what to understand about it.

We've looked at sensations and situations of imbalance: the body emergencies. But what do we experience when we are balanced? Now we turn to the second category of dreams, the Resolved Dream.

Resolved Dreams

In the section on Unresolved Dreams, we looked at stressful situations, challenges, and urgent physical needs. These are only one aspect of our life, however. We also experience beauty, awe, love, and wonder. We gain new perspectives, get inspirations, and—from some mysterious place—have eye-opening ideas. These experiences are reflected in the night dreams called the Great Dream, the Light Dream, and Dreams of Union. These are the Resolved Dreams.

With Resolved Dreams there is no conflict; there's no Necessity to find, because there is nothing to fix. The dream described on page 83—the supernova-like sight in the heavens—is an example. It's just pure experience, whole and balanced.

Though there is no Necessity in Resolved Dreams, there is still a response asked of us. Sometimes they contain a specific message—or evoke one in us—that we need to then make tangible in our waking life. With or without message, though, these dreams dramatically shift our perspective of self. The perspectives they give, and the feelings they confer, change how we view life. This revelation is something to bring into our waking experience by living *differently*. Doing so opens out not only our own lives, but also the lives of those around us, to ever greater possibilities.

As individuals, we are self-organizing systems.[4] When we gain new information, our entire system shifts to incorporate it, making changes on a multitude of levels. This one opened door leads to thousands of open doors in different directions. Now get your calculators out, because the thing is, our self-organizing system is part of the larger self-organizing system of all of life. Whatever new information we receive in a dream that opens a door for us, opens doors of possibility for everyone. Like a newly introduced evolutionary trait in a few individuals that advances the entire species, our ability to *see things differently* puts forward a new idea that is built upon with each life we interact with, and perhaps even beyond.

In the last chapter I wrote about how putting expectation onto dream is a block. A true dreamer receives dreams without expectation, assumption, or values, remaining open to whatever a dream chooses to reveal. I highlight that again here, because our willingness to see the world differently is the determining factor of whether or not we move ourselves into new ways of being and, by extension, that of the whole world. This includes opening oneself to the possibility of being healed of past emotional wounds or current chronic illness as an individual, or living in a peaceful world. So long as we block the reception of the vision of that, we hold ourselves in our current state of being. Because each of us, as individuals, are an active part of the larger whole, each of us is a gateway to evolution.

Resolved Dreams help us to envision beyond our daily expectations. The extraordinary quality of Resolved Dreams startles us into seeing more than what is just in front of us, and what we think we know. It provokes us to go deeper and to engage in mystery. It also opens our eyes to the mystery that surrounds us in the most ordinary of moments. Life events may or may not change on the surface after one of these dreams—we may have the same job, partner, and house—but everything will be different because these same things will be infused with a different sense of meaning and possibility.

Sharing and hearing Great Dreams is an important part of our communal evolution because it opens us to wider possibilities of what life can be. For both dreamer and listener, though, we have to take care not to diminish or shut down the extraordinary aspects of them. As listeners, we must remain as open as we would as a dreamer. Think of it like holding a perfect, iridescent bubble on the tip of the finger, being careful not to disturb and pop it.

Here is an example of a Great Dream, and what happened when it was told to a group.

I step out the back door of a nondescript house in a nondescript housing complex and turn right, taking a path that leads me through increasingly beautiful, amazing homes, distinctive in their character. I turn right again, and there is a

Mexican food restaurant on my right, with a young girl who is the hostess and welcomes me in. All is bright and filled with families and music and amazing food. It smells so good!

I leave with an elegant man and woman on each side of me, maybe from another era, continuing up the path on the right which is now through an incredible street of the most incredible architecture, both Austrian Baroque and modern, shiny skyscrapers. The man and woman both have extremely shiny, thick, beautiful black hair. I notice the woman, who is on my left, has an incredible ring that is like a huge egg and is black as obsidian. I stare closer at it and then look up.

Suspended in front of us, bridging the two sides of the street, is the most incredible building I've ever seen. It is incredibly complex, with many angles and sides, and is built of a dark smoky-colored glass—like some incredibly complex crystal rising up. One horizontal silver line is underneath, stretching and connecting the two sides of the street with this suspended structure above.

Great Dreams are larger-than-life experiences, and this is clearly not a "regular" kind of dream—just note the repetition of the word "incredible." Great Dreams are also characterized by vivid, usually jewel-like, colors. In this one, the vividness of the colors is found in the lustrous black. Black—deep black—repeats in this dream. We find it especially prominent in the shiny black hair, the black ring, and the dark smoky glass of the crystal-like structure. We also find vividness in the bright music, colors, and flavors of the Mexican restaurant. However, the truly extraordinary color here is the black: "black as obsidian."

Black is not a color many would immediately associate with a Great Dream, and it was this that tricked one of the listeners in the group. She commented "I don't like the black—so I wonder, what colors could I make the structure be?" This person allowed an intellectual idea of black—black as a *symbol* of something negative—to pull her away from the overall experience of both *this* black and *this* black in *this* context. She misunderstood the dream and came dangerously close to minimizing someone's experience, as well as closing off possibilities within herself.

We talked about the problem of symbols in Chapter Two. Projecting our own mental constructs onto someone else's images and dreams, rather than feeling them from a sensing, embodied place not only causes us to misunderstand what the dreamer is trying to tell us, it crosses a boundary, inserting our opinions into their subjective world. Imagine, instead, black from an embodied place in this dream, stepping into the shoes of the dreamer and seeing the ring, the jewel shaped like an egg, "black as obsidian," and leaning down to see it more clearly. "Black as obsidian" takes us to a reflective deep place. Peering into it opens us to a mysterious beyond as if peering into the black depths of the universe itself. It's from this mystery depth that things are born, and we are clued in to this because the jewel is shaped like an egg; indeed, just after getting closer to see this, the dreamer sees a crystal structure that is also transparent black.

Being responsive to the dreaming dialogue includes opening ourselves to the mystery of what we don't know yet, even if it counters our prevailing points of view. *Especially* if it counters our current perspectives. This and only this allows us to transform.

Like the woman who made the negative comment about the color black in the Great Dream, we tend to rush to shut down experiences that appear opposite to what we think we know. In creativity research, this is called "premature closure," which is the refusal to explore emergent possibilities, like seeing a drinking glass and saying its only use is to hold liquid. Stopping there at the first evident solution closes the event, instead of opening it out by sitting in the space of non-definition. If we resist defining the glass so quickly, we might discover it can be turned upside-down and used to draw circles, cut mini-tart forms out of dough, or amplify sound through walls.

When a Resolved Dream lifts us out of how we assume the world works, or how we view ourselves and the lives we are living, we have a choice to remain open to it or limit it. This has enormous ramifications. If, for example, in waking time, you've shut down the possibility of finding a relationship because of past wounds, do you stop there, or do you allow your heart to experience love again? Resolved Dreams know this is possible, and often expanded sensations like love are what we sense in them.

All dreams put us in the place of direct experience. In Light Dreams, for example, we experience light with all of our senses, not simply vision. There is no mental thought between us and this sensorial experience. There's no explaining, no filtering, just experiencing. With Resolved Dreams this is highlighted because Light Dreams and Dreams of Union usually lack form and other things we associate with the familiar of everyday. If we open ourselves to the non-familiar experience of these dreams, then our dream and waking lives will be fuller, enriched by expanded ways of being.

When Resolved Dreams contain a message, we have the choice to remain open, and therefore responsive, or not. A client had two Great Dreams just a few days apart that indicated she should call—just call—a man that she knew of through friends but hadn't interacted with personally. She stayed open and called him. They decided to meet, and today they are married. Her message was ultra-specific, but other times the message simply stimulates an inner knowing, like "it's time to do that next thing," or "the degree program that is right for me is the one in New York." We'll look more closely at how to work with the messages of Great Dreams in Chapter Ten.

Revelation is, inherently, at odds with the status quo. The status quo of life is generally that of routine, conflict, fear, and doubt—the grist of Unresolved Dreams. What is revelatory is that other ways of being are also possible. Part of working with dreams is to learn to allow newness, to be open to strange and unexpected ideas, perspectives, and potentials. To build a better self and world, we have to accept these revelatory possibilities without sullying them with the fears and doubts of daily life. Human evolution depends on having these dreams and being open to their messages. They provide us with a new image for a future we can begin building now.

Dreaming and Response

A Nightmare, waiting for us to engage with it, a Great Dream asking us to live it. Dreams are not inert phenomena; they are dialoguing with us, and that dialogue asks for a response. What response, and how, is aided by sorting dream experiences into the type of dream and the category of Resolved or Unresolved. We looked at how Resolved Dreams require us to be open to new experiences and possibly respond to a message. With Unresolved Dreams we respond by interacting with them directly to shift them from unbalanced to a state of resolution. This same tool can be applied to waking life experience.

We start with our night dreams. Once you've written your dream in the morning, ask yourself if something feels "not right," "unbalanced," "unfinished," or "off." If so, you've just sorted the dream into one of the four Unresolved Dreams. If everything feels complete, and there is no sign of conflict in any part of the dream, then you've had a Resolved Dream.

I've rarely had people question what type of dream they've had, especially if it's a Resolved Dream, because the experience is so different. If you have a question about your dream, though, go back through it and see if perhaps there was the presence of something that wasn't balanced at one point in the dream, but then resolved within the dream itself. If so, it's still an Unresolved Dream. In this case, rather than working with the dream material itself, the response the dream is needing will likely be acting upon the dream to bring resolve to the issue in waking time.

Once you've determined if your dream is resolved or unresolved, decide which kind of dream you've had. It's helpful to look at the colors of the dream, like we did in Chapter Three. Nightmares, for example, will often consist of dark colors, blood reds, and blacks. These are the colors of intense emotions, and correspond to the sensed experience of a waking Nightmare situation—for example, seeing red when very angry. Everyday colors, with maybe a bright color or a colorful object, tell us we're having a Clear Dream; just like in daily life, a colorful punctuation speaks to potential that is waiting to be found.

It helps to sort through dreams at the end of the day, when you have a bit of distance from your waking, immediate, felt sense of the dream, and any emotions or associations that might have arisen with it. While this waking, dreamy, reflective space is fantastic for meaning-making, idea-capturing, and visioning, the end of the day gives us a new lens for rolling up our sleeves to do the more objective work of finding what is out of order and repairing it.

So now, let's say you've had an Unresolved Dream. The next step is to identify the conflict and the Necessity. Remember, there may be many things wrong in the dream, but there is only one Necessity, which means all the conflicts can boil down to one main issue. Think of a toilet overflowing—there's dirty water everywhere in the room, but the main issue is the blockage in the pipe in the toilet. We can try to clean up the water in the room, but it won't help anything until the pipe gets unblocked.

Start by simply naming every conflict that you see. The dream with the car heading to a gaping hole had numerous conflicts: too many people, too-loud music, driving too fast, road too dark, gaping hole up ahead. Of these five things, four are more or less the same: too much of something. That makes clear that the gaping hole is more consequence than conflict. I can imagine removing some of the people, but the music will still be too loud, the car will still be going too fast, the road too dark. We would run into the same issue if we only tried to turn down the music, or any one of the other singular conflicts. Instead, we have to look at the entire suite of conflicts and name it. We can name the conflict in this Nightmare as "too much." That makes clear that the Necessity is "stop." Like the water in the overflowing toilet example, the conflicts or the gaping hole may be where my attention goes, but the real problem—the cause—is underneath it.

Once you put your finger on the Necessity then you can go back to the dream and respond to it, like I did with the client who had the car dream. In that dream the Necessity was to stop the car, which we did by a Waking Dream exercise. To do that I had the client close her eyes, do a short breathing exercise, and imagine returning to the dream and see and feel herself get back into the car and stop it.

Here is how you do it for your own dream Necessity: Close your eyes, and let your breathing return to its normal rhythm. Then, on an exhale, breathe out seeing the number three. On the next exhale see the number two. On the next exhale see the number one: tall, clear, and very bright.

Then, imagine that you return to the moment in the dream that needs to be resolved, and make the change that you identified as needing to be made. Once you do, the images will change. If all feels resolved, then on your next exhale open your eyes. If another step is needed, just stay in response to the images, interacting with them, until all return to balance. Once balanced, exhale and open your eyes.

When interacting with a dream in this way, remember that you have all the tools in your imagination at your service. In the car dream, the client gets into the driver's seat and pushes the brake. Instantly everything returns to calm. In other Waking Dream exercises the images might ask for a new step: one example may be freeing a prisoner from a dungeon, which transforms the prisoner from rags to shiny clothes and health, only to have the king, who put him there in the first place, appear to block the exit. All that is needed is to stay in response to the images—no thinking! You might ask the king what he needs and respond. If it is a masked man who jumps in the path, unmask him. If it's a box blocking the way, find a way over, around, under, or through. These are just suggestions. If you listen to the feelings in your own body *(The king wants payment from me*; *Who is behind the mask?*; *The box is in my way)* and stay in response to the images, you will know what to do. It is the difference between moving instinctively versus thinking.

Like the gaping hole car crash dream, our complicated modern lives have a lot of moving parts. We have work deadlines, duties to keep the household running, exigencies for our personal physical health, and relationships with family, friends, and co-workers. There may be more than one conflict in these different areas, and pinpointing an exact root cause can be difficult. Looking at waking life as a dream can help. Figuring out what category a certain experience belongs to, and which type of "dream" it is, helps you identify what needs to be worked on or transformed.

Start by taking an episode in your life, like a team meeting, and write it down. Put every single detail there that you think of. Let a day pass and then look at it as a dream. Use the steps we've used so far to know if it is unresolved or resolved, then decide what kind of dream it is. If unresolved, then take a look at the different areas of conflict, and underline or highlight them so they stand out clearly. It helps, too, to then say them out loud and hear yourself as you say them. Then, name the conflict. One tip is to see what issue or word recurs (think of how we pinpointed the way so many aspects of the out-of-control car dream were described as "too much"). That should make both the Necessity and the resolve clear.

I gave an example in Chapter Three of the client who was having a Busy Dream experience in waking life. A management shift had tangled his energies and he arrived to our session feeling he was about to be fired and needed help finding a new job. His many conflicts included a "bad manager," a team that he "couldn't trust," an "aging" problem, an associated "retirement plan" issue, and so on. These symptoms really did go on and on, and I recognized all this as the piling on of emotion found in a Busy Dream. Once I had that figured out, I knew to ask questions until we got to the bottom of the pile, which turned out to be the change to new management and a resulting obligation to learn a new computer program. Rather than excoriate the manager, find a new job, or any other of his proposed, panic-driven "fixes," the real Necessity was to ask for help in learning the new program. Simple. And it saved him his job.

Another example is the client who came to a session saying "I'm not ready," followed by a panicked tally of all the experience and skills he was lacking to "move to the next step." I heard in this a Nightmare and could describe it as "frozen in place." What was extra curious was that he started the session with a stop—"I'm not ready"—without further details. So, I asked, "Not ready for what?" It turns out that there was something specific: a really great job offer! The panic this job offer set off had even caused this client to omit this very important detail in our conversation.

He's not alone. I call this "burying the lede," a phrase from journalism, where the main headline gets stuck several paragraphs down at the end of the article. Burying the lede is frequent; the emotional alarm set off in reaction to a change or event takes the stage and kicks the important aspects of what is actually going on way down the line. But remember, Nightmares are *acute* emotion, like the panicked, full-stop of this client. They're not like the diffused emotion of a Busy Dream presented by the guy thinking he needed to get a new job. So even though the panicked client buried the lede, the acute emotion made distinguishing the experience easy.

Now I had the full picture: the client/dreamer was *frozen in place*, unable to get (or even see) the treasure that awaited just ahead. The Necessity? *Move!*

Frozen in place has to return to motion. In this case, *Move!* looked like calling back the company who had made the offer and accepting the job, something he had, astonishingly, been sitting on for days.

The simple act of learning to describe is often a solution itself. In the case of the dancer dream in Chapter Three, the dreamer in waking life immediately shifted out of fear upon realizing she was able to dance and jump in the flow despite her anxieties. This realization put her in a clear space. She already had the tools. Without even doing a waking dream exercise, her choice was near-automatic: "I'm going to keep dancing and creating."

Pausing to describe our lived experiences, and to note which kind of dream we are dreaming, not only helps us tease out actual conflict and know how to respond to it, it can guide our focus to possibilities that are already present but need to be acted on.

There's more to dreams than just their types and categories, they are also deeply meaningful and rich in content. We've already had glimpses of that in the dreams we've looked at, but in the next chapter we go deeper into how to know what our dreams are telling us.

CHAPTER FIVE

Beyond Story to Deeper Meaning: The Four Levels of Dreaming

"Here I go again. It's the same thing, over and over. Just when I thought I had found someone new, the same old story starts all over again."

—Dreamer 1

"I feel like I've been down this road before. Yes. This is a road I am quite familiar with."

—Dreamer 2

An out-of-control car that is not just about a car, an obstructing box that is more than a box. In the last few chapters, we've been looking at dreams and images that have meanings that go far beyond what they seem on the surface. Already, sorting dreams into their different kinds and determining if they are resolved or unresolved helps us dip below the first glance at a dream. In this chapter, we are going to go even deeper—four levels deep, in fact.

Dreams start with a story. Even if a dream is a simple image, the way we describe that image, and the way we tell the experience of it, is the story. **Story, or *peshat*,** is the first level of dreams. It is what you write down in your dream journal: the literal, simple meaning of things. At this level of dream, a car is a car, and a box is still just a box.

The second level of dreams is the level of **Pattern, or *remes*.** Pattern shows us what is repeating in a dream. It may be the repetition of words and phrases, or the appearance of a repeated theme, movement, color, or an object. We've encountered this already, too, in the repetition of the "so" many people and "too" loud music of the car Nightmare, and the "finishing" of the house to be renovated.

Pattern in a dream flags our attention. Like the ground crew at an airport waving flags to direct the plane into the right gate, patterns turn our view from the literal to what lies beyond it. They are the ultimate *hint hint, wink wink* that drives us to ask questions about a dream's meaning. When we take the hint of patterns, we start to wonder *why* something is repeating. Repetition is a version of highlighting something or giving it exclamation points. It's important, and it's saying something quite specific—we want to know what.

The third level of dreams looks to understand the message of the patterns, and it does it by asking questions. We call it the level of **Question, or *drash*.** In the level of *drash*, we start to walk around the pattern, look over and under it, and lift the hood to see what the highlighting of pattern is all about. We ask questions about where the patterns appear: Does a pattern show up after the same sequence of events, with a repeating origin event that kicks it off? Or does the pattern highlight or accentuate what is missing? Maybe a dream contains a pattern in which we can only eat apples and it makes us wonder what other things can appear—bananas or oranges—if we get away from just apples.

We get curious, too, about *how* something is repeating. To use an example from a client's dream, we can look at the appearance of an old white shirt stretched over an old fat man's belly in the first part of the dream that, later in the dream, becomes a shining, white overcoat on Bill Clinton. Here is a pattern of large men, white clothing, and "over," but one is old and stretched, while the other is shining and suits the size of the man wearing it. The *why* behind this difference sends us looking again at the dream with a next round of questions.

The level of *drash* explores what the various patterns of the dream are indicating. It's also the level of connecting the dots. It is through questions—unpacking patterns and sensing what the images of the patterns are telling us—that we come to understand the overall dialogue of the dream.

That understanding leads us to the fourth level, the level of **Mystery, or *sod*.** We have no idea what will be unlocked within us when we understand the deeper elements of the dream. Dreaming is holistic, and it speaks to our whole selves. Whatever understanding we may grasp from a particular dream will resonate with many facets of our lives. In the level of *sod*, 2+2 is never 4, but something infinite. At this level, we encounter the mystery of our Self and what lies beyond a surface view of life. We sense meaning and a deep connection to Source and Other.

Here is a dream example for us to work with to see this in action:

> *I am with Jake in a room I don't know. It seems that we have already spent some time here. It's like a hostel—two bunk beds, with two windows. Jake is leaving the space, and I decide to stay behind. I am cleaning the room and I find a plastic bag where there is old food. It's mainly leftovers of a dairy product. It looks white and liquid. I try to clean the*

bag. There are two sinks next to each other. They're beautiful sinks, really clean, antiseptic.

I use one sink and think of also using the other one. When I lift up the plug on the drain, I see that there are growing sprouts, like soy sprouts, on it. It disgusts me a bit, and I'm worried I can't use it anymore. Then I see red peppers growing in the water pipe. This fascinates me and is nice. I stop cleaning to look. There are two—one little pepper and one big pepper.

I am sitting with Jake on the curb. Alice passes by. She says she has to stay in isolation. I'm sad for her and leave Jake to accompany her to her house. The mother opens the door. I have never seen her before. She looks younger than I expected her to be. She is very pretty, and she just woke up. In the back I can hear music, like Spanish salsa music. They are dancing. I like it. Alice's cousin joins the situation. They haven't seen each other for some time. I stand in the doorway. I feel attracted to the cousin, and I am a bit jealous that she's spending the time now with Alice. They are hugging and seem super cozy and familiar. The whole situation makes me feel outside. I don't feel sad for Alice anymore. I am jealous and would like to join.

What you've just read is the level of Story, or *peshat*. Now, like a camera that adjusts its focus, we click in a level deeper to notice the patterns. The story of this dream is replete with them.

The first obvious pattern is the repetition of two: two beds, two windows, two sinks, two peppers. The words "sad" and "jealous" repeat twice. Now return to the dream and look at it again.

Even at this initial point of noticing patterns, has anything changed in the way you understand it?

Other elements of this dream repeat. We see the aspect of Jake in two parts of the dream. In both parts, there is a movement of being with Jake, or having been together, and separating, with one part remaining behind: in the beginning, Jake is leaving and the dreamer remains, alone, and cleans. In the second appearance, Jake is present and the dreamer leaves Jake to accompany Alice, who remains in isolation. Notice that in both cases, the dreamer makes a decision—*chooses*—to separate from Jake and be alone. Return to the dream again. What, now, is becoming clear?

Let's look at these red peppers. Later in the dream there is salsa music. Red peppers make salsa. This is a play on words, from salsa music to salsa dipping sauce, and dreams love to use puns and other wordplay to help us find the patterns. Further, the red peppers are discovered underneath, below something else; the salsa is back behind, "in the back" of the house. There is a little pepper and behind it a big pepper; there is Alice and behind her, opening the door, her mother—little and big again. With the peppers, something is growing in a hidden place; specifically, the dreamer says "sprouts." Remembering how we read image, what is the quality of pepper and salsa (music or sauce)? I feel them as peppy, spicy, energetic. And "sprouts" —we can read it as a verb. Return again to the dream. What, now, are you understanding, even at just this second level?

Patterns are most easily found by searching for repeating words and phrases. When you work with your own dreams, start by reading the story of the dream. Reading out loud always helps, because our ears often pick up repetitions that our eyes flit over. Then, take a moment to go through the dream and underline any repeating words or phrases. Once you've done that, read all that you've underlined out loud, in the order they appear, as if they are a poem. For example, *two-two, Jake leaving, decide stay behind, two pepper pepper*. This step, like a poem, helps us to not only hear the pattern more clearly, we also hear the beats and rhythms of it, which helps us catch changes.

Spending time on the level of Pattern sifts through details of the dream, separating trees from forest and bringing salient aspects to the visible surface. The moment we do that, questions start to arise. I have a lot of questions around this dream, so now that we've viewed the dream through the lens of Pattern, let's move to the third level of dreaming, *drash*, or Question, and see what the pattern is showing us.

My first curiosity is around Jake. The dreamer has been traveling with Jake, but when Jake keeps moving, the dreamer stays behind. Remember that every aspect of the dream is an aspect of the dreamer. So, to say that differently, one aspect of the dreamer is in movement and continues to go new places; one stagnates. The one in movement leaves a closed, inner space to go out; the other stays in. Later, the dreamer is with Jake again but leaves to follow an aspect of the dream, Alice, who has to stay in isolation. Isolation is another type of closed, inner space. It is also stagnation. Jake moves, but the dreamer/Alice is stuck.

Reading image, we know that both Jake and Alice are an aspect of the dreamer. Because these are actual people in waking life, as opposed to a red pepper, we ask a specific question to understand the quality of this aspect. The question here is what aspect of the dreamer is Jake reflecting? To find out, we ask the dreamer to finish the sentence: "Jake is the kind of person who. . . " Whatever immediate impressions come out is the aspect of that person presenting at that moment in time. When asked about Jake, the dreamer said, "He's very warm-hearted." Now we put that together to see the pattern and get to the real question: the dreamer steps away two times from the warmth and movement of her heart. Why?

At this point, we get to play detective, reading the images and putting the pieces together. Because images are embodied, our first step is to return to the initial scenario: what is the *felt sense* of this space? Ordered, antiseptic. The dreamer remains there, as one, but the room is organized for two (two beds, two windows, two sinks). The motive? To clean. Ordered, antiseptic—which feels a lot like sterile, clean. As a detective, this doesn't add up if I compare it to the warm heart of Jake. How does the heart move? Hearts, and love, are rather emotional, at times even messy; their ways are ever-changing and rarely ordered or controlled. The warmth of the heart moves us to new places, like relationships going to a next step. Now we have a clearer picture of the scene. Jake, the warmth of the emotional heart, continues moving. The dreamer stays behind to be alone and clean the traces of their time together.

What else characterizes the space of ordered, antiseptic, clean? Ostensibly nothing grows here, but the lifting of the plug in the sink reveals sprouts growing in a hidden place. *I lift the plug*. This means the dreamer has *previously plugged something up*. Another stagnation. What? Under the plug are sprouts and two red peppers. We read sprouts as the embodied sense of something rising up and growing—the beginning of something new. The red peppers are spicy and red, like the heart, and even shaped as such. They're warm, like the aspect of Jake. Two peppers, two hearts: the dreamer and Jake. Stepping into the question of this dream, and the shoes of the dreamer, we might ask: *When I feel the first sprouting of passion and love, something that can move into relationship, do I plug it up?*

Now we can follow this action like breadcrumbs in the forest. The peppers appear in the first part of the dream as a burst of color in a white space, next as a burst of movement, dancing, and noise with the salsa music. Where is the dancing? Behind an initially closed door—a second "plug." But what are the effects of the pepper element? In the first scene, the peppers fascinate, and draw the dreamer closer to look. In the second, the salsa music wakes up the mother, and opens the door. In both cases, stagnation is reversed by the peppers; they are the aspect that sparks things to move in a different direction. *Can heat, passion, heart, and movement unplug and open a door to Other?*

The pepper aspect opens doors and hearts to others, and yet, in the second part of the dream, the dreamer stands in the doorway, just outside. Outside, here, is not only outside the door of the house, it is outside the circle of warmth, "hugging," and "coziness" of the family. The dreamer even says explicitly in the dream that they *feel* outside.

The dream says family. Remember, though, dreams love wordplay. We can read this as *familiar*, which is another way to say pattern. Patterns are the stable thing we know, because we've lived it already enough times that we recognize it. That's why patterns are hard to see in our waking time because we are so accustomed to them. This is the tricky thing about patterns: even if they work to our disadvantage, they are hard to let go of because they are, in some way, comfortable. This is why working with dreams is such a useful tool for illuminating them.

At this point in the dream, we fully move to the third level of deeper meaning because we've made it beyond the kicking-the-tires work of looking at the different patterns and now see the big picture of what these patterns are saying about the dreamer's waking life. It comes down to the *feeling* of outside, the *sense* of being an outsider.

Feeling like an outsider, one aspect of the dreamer is choosing to separate from the heart, to stay solo in isolation instead of relating to others. The dreamer's aspect that stays outside is the patterned aspect. This is a tricky pattern, because the dreamer may think, in waking life, that they are not accepted by others, and that being alone is a *consequence* of others' actions. However, the dream shows us that it is not relationships that have separated from this dreamer. The door is open. Everything is available to them. It is that the dreamer has chosen to separate from the relationships. "I decide to stay behind." "I choose to leave Jake." It's this *choice* of remaining outside, when inclusion is available, that is the familiar. *The self that feels outside chooses to stay outside.*

We often feel that we "have no choice but. . . " or that "this is how things are." These are both statements flagging pattern. Patterns seem *logical.* Because in one way or another they seem to have worked before, so they are the preferred approach for our logical-thinking mind. We even see this in the dream, with the Alice aspect that *has* to stay in isolation. This logical mind is causal, remember (A+B=C, *always*). It's the default network, the dreaming mechanism, that moves us out of this causal chain by helping us to imagine beyond what our logical mind thinks is obvious.

The dream we are working with shows us that there are other options than choosing to stay behind. In fact, the dream does this by illustrating that these contradictory aspects are already present within. Because all aspects of the dream are aspects of the dreamer, this dreamer contains a warm heart and the potential for relationship. These very elements, in their sensory aspects—*spicy, movement, salsa, dancing, hugging, cozy*—evoke the body memory of experience beyond the pattern. That jolt gets the dreamer to pay attention, letting loose possibility. Remember that when seeing the red pepper, the dreamer says "this fascinates me and is nice," which causes them to look closer. Ultimately, it is the sensory elements that give way to the desire to do something different—*I am attracted to the cousin, I would like to join.* This embodied desire opens the door to the part of the dreamer that is staying behind and outside.

Desire and the body's inner knowing bring us to a new place, the fourth level of dream: *sod,* or Mystery. It is the tantalizing *what if* that lies on the other end of possibility. What if the dreamer opens the door to their heart and enters a relationship? What if we dare to step out of pattern that keeps us isolated, feeling outside, and acting out in jealousy and self-pity? What if we move from the position of victim to agent?

The logic of the thinking mind works with past events and patterns, driven by causality. Dreaming is a different kind of thinking, an "a-logic,"[1] noncausal cognition. Rather than thinking in causal links, which are chained together, dreaming works with analogies and synthesizes disparate pieces of experience, memory, and knowledge to arrive at new configurations. These are the so-called bizarre elements in dreams—bizarre, only because we are used to seeing what we already expect. It's this dreaming cognition that allows us to envision beyond the patterns of personal history. By bringing us back to the truth of our bodies, we encounter the vast background against which a handful of challenging events is only a small piece. Returning to this expanded self we access the many other experiences we've had in life beyond those few challenging ones that keep us locked in place. This frees us to use these other parts of the self to break the patterns and create a different life trajectory.

The Mystery level of dreams is the revelation that comes when moving beyond story, through patterns, and asking the right questions. It is where our meaning-making of the dream stretches into our waking life. Working with the dream and revealing the pattern that has been directing a certain waking way of seeing and acting, will change the dreamer's perspective. That change will inherently shift the external fabric of the dreamer's waking life, and different life choices will become apparent. It is here that we make the connections between the elements revealed in the dream and the bigger picture of one's life. We are never the same, subtle or dramatic as it may be, after working with a dream. The level of Mystery contains the question of what the dreamer, in waking life, will do now.

After working with this dream, the dreamer said they were currently learning a new language in waking life: Spanish. The soy sprouts took on new meaning: *soy* is Spanish for *I am*. The dreamer understood that the *new language* is the one proposed by the dream, uncovering the essential, sprouting I AM. This I AM for the dreamer is what the warm heart really speaks to: love. The new language of love means loving all aspects of the Self, as well as being available to loving relationships with others. Recognizing that "I am love" and "I am in relationship"—now, with all others in the world—became the healing rebuttal to the old pattern of "I am outsider."

The Four Levels in Waking Life

The dream we've just worked with is a Clear Dream. Here's how we get there. First, we see it is unresolved. It contains elements of conflict: separateness, isolation, sadness, jealousy, feeling outside. However, it also contains elements of potential: Jake and the warm heart, unplugging, fascination, sprouts, peppers, salsa, dance, hugging. It's definitely not a Nightmare. Not only does it contain potential, the colors are everyday colors, including one color that stands out as very pronounced: the red pepper. It's not a Busy Dream, because the story is coherent. That leaves us with a Clear Dream.

Clear Dreams lay out where we are in our current state. In this case, the current state of the dreamer is plugged, outside, isolated, jealous; static, because the dreamer had *been* traveling with Jake. This means that before the block, the dreamer was fluidly traveling with the warm heart aspect of the self. In addition to the block, Clear Dreams also show us where we can go, which in this dream is back to traveling, moving in the world, with the heart. Not only unplugging, stepping in, dancing, and hugging, but also, more deeply, embracing the I AM that is, at its base, love. Both capable of loving and being loved. This choice between block or potential is the quantum moment of Clear Dreams. If we make a choice to activate what is potential, we collapse the wave of pattern and allow our energy to re-form in a new configuration.

Just as we worked in a previous chapter to ascribe the scenarios of our waking life to one of the seven kinds of dreams, we can also apply the four levels to our waking experience. This helps us to not only understand what we are dreaming, but to move beyond now to what *can be*. Without conscious examination, waking life rests at the level of story, the linear telling of what we are living and experiencing. But life is so much more than that. We sense it, and using the four levels, we can consciously explore it.

The chapter opens with two excerpts. Go back and look at them. One is from waking life, and one is from a dream. Can you tell which is which? It's hard to do, which illustrates how seamless our waking and dreaming experiences really are. One talks about a *same old story*, the other *a road I've been down before*. Notice that both of these talk about the repetition of something. This is clearly speaking to the second level of Pattern.

Patterns create their own mental reasoning in different situations, usually found in emotional justifications. In the dream of the red pepper, the choice to stay in isolation, to not engage, sets the patterned dreamer outside. In reaction to this choice, the messy emotions of feeling sorry for the self, and feeling jealous of others who are in warm relationships, arise. The dreamer says this of the Alice aspect that has to stay in isolation: *I'm sad for her*.

In waking life, we can use these emotional statements to help us track backwards until we get to the pattern. Not only do these statements appear in our mental thoughts, like *nobody will like me*, they show up in our conversations with others. We often call friends to tell a story about something that has upset us, or a difficulty we are having. The next time you do so, pay attention to emotional sensations that arise, either in feeling or in actual words, like *jealous*. Catch it and look at the conversation around it. Try to summarize it like you would a movie, for example: *The dreamer is jealous because they think others are in relationship and wish they had one for themselves.*

Our patterns play out with people and events that camouflage them as being discrete happenings, when in fact they've been happening exactly the same way in different situations for a while. When we step back and approach them as a dream, scratching below the surface of names and details, the *felt sense* reveals itself, such as that of being outsider. Then, we can ask ourselves when else we've had this feeling. If we see it at numerous key moments of challenge in our lives, then we've hit the pattern.

We can avoid the trap of Story, which is the surface-level understanding of what is happening, by recognizing that the events of daily life are just the first level; we need to move deeper into these events, through all four levels of dream. That may only require putting our finger on Pattern. Pattern tells us immediately that there are other perspectives available; apples-apples-apples does not mean that there are only apples, but it clues us in that something exists outside apples that we can get curious about and explore.

I worked with one client who told me a long story about her mother moving back in, and that it added so much extra work to her already-full schedule because she had to clean and cook for her. The key word here is *had*. I asked one question: Why? She got really quiet—for a long time!—then replied, "I didn't even know I said that." That's the thing about patterns, they've been there so long they become as invisible as the air we breathe. With this pause and reflection, suddenly, we had a rich session to look at all the *had*s from present to childhood and realize that underneath was the pattern of *doing everything for my mother*. Why? As the story went, "because otherwise she won't love me." This realization opened out an entire new beginning in her communication with her mother, and subsequent enriching of their relationship. The irritations of "had" gave way to enjoying her mother's presence and even appreciating the extra help with the kids.

Emotions, like this client's irritation, are symptoms of pattern and we can treat them as such; rather than wasting time on chasing them, we can move beyond them to the actual cause. Irritation and jealousy are lower-grade emotions, unlike the sharpness of anger or fear, and so usually this tells us we are dreaming a Clear Dream and not a Nightmare. Another approach we can take, then, is by remembering that Clear Dreams signal not only block but potential; outside the "symptoms" we experience around pattern, we can find the latent possibility that we're skipping over. When we cultivate a practice of seeking out and exploring other perspectives, we safeguard ourselves from falling into a pattern in the first place.

And then there's the level of Question. We go deeper still into our waking lives by listening to our inner dialogue, hearing the questions that our actions bring up. Many clients come to me with these questions already in mind, things like, *Why am I always getting passed over by promotions*? Or, *Why do my relationships start great and end quickly?* Getting curious about these patterns means objectively walking around them as we did with the dream, looking at where they appear, what events precede them, and what emotions and felt sensations accompany them. When the facts have been gathered, sit quietly and let the primary question arise. This will bring you to a new place of understanding, the Mystery level (*sod*).

In an earlier chapter, I suggested an exercise of choosing a waking life event and writing it down to work with it as a dream. That's a great practice to do again, here, to practice with the four levels. What you write down as the literal recounting of that event as you would tell a friend or a partner is important in order to hear the story you're telling. While Story is only the first level, you may find that STORY is where you spend a lot of time. When we are stuck in a pattern, we have a specific story around it that we tend to nurture.

We get quite invested in our patterns, and seeing the story written on paper helps to put our finger on it and deal with it at arm's length. Underlining the repeating words and phrases, identifying sensations and emotions, and then asking questions gives us further remove from taking it so personally, in addition to helping us work with it. That remove will then be our best help in finding new perspectives and stepping out of the restriction of story and pattern, and into the expansion of being.

In this chapter, we looked at the four levels of dreams and how to apply them to waking life. Not just a tool to transform our many patterns, this rubric helps us penetrate the superficial to access meaning in our lives. Each of the names of the four levels – *peshat*, *remes*, *drash*, and *sod* – create the acronym of prds, which means, in the original Hebrew language, orchard or paradise.[2] By recognizing that which lies beneath the surface of things, learning to step outside of story and pattern, one reaches a deeper, quieter space in the Self; go all the way and we find the blossoming and fruiting of an orchard, the harmony of paradise. Life, no longer flat and repetitive, erupts in color and dimension.

While looking at patterns, we saw how difficult it is to recognize them. The next chapter focuses in on that, looking specifically at how dreams work to trick us into seeing clearly.

CHAPTER SIX

"I'm in a..."

"I am in a car going way too fast." "I am in a dance workshop." "I am with Jake in a room I don't know." Almost every dream begins with "I'm in a. . . " In one dream you may be attending a loud party, while another night you may dream in a quiet meadow.

Dreaming, as we've discussed, is the language of our experiencing; images are experience made tangible. In addition, all dreams, all images, are present tense, putting a finger on a particular moment in experience, catching it by a visual tail so we can perceive and apprehend it. All aspects of dream speak to this right-now experience—not just the dreamer interacting with the dream, but also the sensual geography of the dream itself, the mise-en-scène in which we find ourselves.

In waking time, we introduce our perceptual background by saying things like "I'm in such a good mood today" or "I feel a little blue." Dreams, however, give us much more detail than the shortcut phrases we use in verbal conversation. They put us, for example, in the audience of a concerto, or in a modern city with tall buildings. These locations aren't just a *where*, they are the full, sensory experience of also what and how. The warm-toned lights and relaxed harmony of the concerto feel horizontal, like a cozy circle, while the sleek steel and glass of the city is sharper and reaches high in the vertical zone. These locations become images that we can read, just as we've been reading other images in this book. Warm and cozy is a very different state of being than sleek and reaching high.

The "I'm in a. . . " phrase that kicks off most dreams is what I call the **Locating Aspect** of images in dreams. It is exposition to the dreamer's present tense. Whatever details follow this phrase—the location and all of its specific characterizations—provide the physical, emotional, mental, and spiritual starting point of the dreamer's experience. This Locating Aspect is the first idea to keep in mind in this chapter.

If the Locating Aspect is like the key to a musical piece, guiding us to the mood and tempo, the rest of the details are its notes. Remember, every aspect of the dream is an aspect of the dreamer, and this includes the orientating location, everything that populates it, as well as everything that happens within and after it. Within this symphony of details are different viewpoints, held not only by the "I" of the dream, but also other characters, even objects, that are present. The "I" is self, but so are the other aspects of the dream. Like being part of a group, this "I" is both among and set opposite to the other aspects and their viewpoints. Sometimes these other aspects are in harmony with the "I," but they might also hold divergent positions. This is where dreams get tricky.

Let's say I dream I'm at a garden party with a woman sitting by a round pool, under a bright yellow umbrella, waiting for her partner to come. "I," however, stand off to the side in a second pool which is dry, narrow, rectangular, and only made for swimming laps. The woman by the watery pool, as well as the round pool and the bright yellow umbrella, is as valid a perspective as is the "I" of the dream that is standing to the side in the dry, rectangular lap pool. The "I," however, feels agency. Because it recognizes itself as "itself," as in "me," it directs the dream. Herein lies the possible trick.

This dream is from a client, and it is at this moment in the dream that the "I" decides it is not willing to wait for a partner, leaves the dry lap pool, and is suddenly paired with a radical bad boy in an office. A partner at last! But. . . Does the "I" hold the best point of view, or is it a stuck perspective? Is it expressing true agency or acting from pattern? Who is the ultimate decision-maker in the dream?

The "I" of the dream is the part we identify with, that we think of as the self. I call this aspect the **Presenting "I"**. Like the Locating Aspect of "I am in a," the Presenting "I" is also an orientation; in this case, it is the point of view that the dreamer is currently in and is using to direct their waking life at the moment. Hence, the Presenting "I". This waking life point of view gets pulled into the dream, like a starting point and lens for looking at everything else, and against which the other parts of the dream will either contrast or highlight. It has agency and sometimes causes the dreamer to take wrong turns in the dream. It doesn't have the final word, though, because the other aspects of the dream are also weighing in. The Presenting "I" is the second big idea to keep in mind in this chapter.

These other aspects of the dream outside our Presenting "I" are our dreams' tools to help us see beyond the single, limited perspective we are operating from. If we listen to the other aspects, then we enlarge our way of understanding where we are and what is happening to us. But if we wake up and hold too tightly to the Presenting "I", we can trick ourselves out of getting a dream's message. It's easy to do; the agency of this Presenting "I" makes it quite sure of itself, and it holds tightly to patterns. We will get further into the idea of the Presenting "I" in a little bit, on page 131.

Putting a focus to the Locating Aspect of images in dreams and the Presenting "I" helps us move closer to sorting through the myriad images, characters, and viewpoints in dreams, ensuring that we sense into the dream and ask the right questions so that we understand clearly what our dreams are telling us. As with the tools in previous chapters, these two lenses can also be used to explore and shift waking experience. We'll look at both in this chapter.

Location, Location, Location

Let's understand location. Our body is our home. Being in here, in our astronaut skinsuit, is our first cognitive and perceptual experience of in and out;[1] I'm *in me*, with thoughts, emotions, and reflections of my interior space, and objective things happen *out*side me, in the exterior space of the rest of the world. In/out becomes a way of characterizing and sorting things: we are *in* a relationship with someone; we fall *out* of love. We can use it to describe a felt sense or experience, like being *in* awe of something, *in* a certain state of mind, *in* a moment of anger. It might denote a situation or perspective, like finding ourselves *in* a bad team at work; we may show up to coffee with a friend, but still be *in* an argument with our partner *in* our own head.

In tells us a lot about where we find ourselves in our present tense. Denoting interior space, if we are *in* something it is immersive on some level. *In* can also give us a clue as to where we are headed, because wherever we've landed in the moment is not only our location, but the vantage point from which we are viewing all experience. That vantage point directs our looking and therefore our decision-making. We might find ourselves in a moment of fear, for example, which means we will be making choices and acting from this perspective, which will likely be protective, and diminish our capabilities in some way. That perspective can be explored, however. Once we put our finger on our location on our inner map, we immediately see that we can move somewhere else. Maps have a lot of destinations, and fear can become courage, curiosity, steadiness, or something else. To shift perspective, however, we have to first figure out where we are.

Not only does the Locating Aspect give us our present tense, like a starting point on a map—"you are here"—we can also use it to mark movement within the dream. If the dream starts at a heavy metal concert and transitions to a lullaby, we can sense there has been a quieting, a move to resolution. It could also go the other way with the start of a lullaby leading to a heavy metal concert. By having marked the Locating Aspect, and seeing the change, we can then take a look to pinpoint the moment at which something shifts.

In the dancer dream of Chapter Three, the initial orientation was "in a dance workshop." Nearly immediately, the dreamer feels the teacher is going too fast in giving the dance steps, and just after, the dream moves to the tight, traffic-jammed city. From the starting location of being in fluid movement, the dream devolves into stopped traffic. In the red pepper dream of the last chapter the location "with Jake in a room I don't know" led to a choice of staying behind. Split the sentence: "with Jake," there's no problem; progressing to "a room I don't know" kicks off the pattern of dealing with the uncontrollable aspect of relationships.

Let's look at this in a full dream:

I'm in a football game, on the one-yard line. I see the quarterback throw me a perfect toss, but I don't think I am going to catch it. Somehow, I feel I can't move or can't move fast enough. It's like my arms and legs are frozen.

Here, the dreamer is *in* the game; they are active, responsive, moving their life forward—so far forward, in fact, that they are just at the moment of bringing something to fruition, at the one-yard line, about to catch a touchdown pass. Whether it is a waking life challenge or a new step in their inner evolution, they've done the inner and outer work to line everything up to score the goal. They're literally right there, right now—that's the Locating Aspect.

Now the action starts. The first thing that happens in the dream is that the dreaming self as quarterback is giving the dreaming self as receiver the energy and creativity they need to manifest their goal by tossing them the ball. A *perfect* toss. The dreamer/receiver (you'll recognize this as the Presenting "I" in the next section) sees the throw and freezes. The Locating Aspect is "in a place to achieve"; the dreaming perspective is forward movement. However, an old pattern that is not yet aligned with this set-up shifts the initial Locating Aspect to immobilization by the perspective-feeling of self-doubt—*I don't think I am going to catch it.* The dreamer is stuck, right at the point of potential achievement. And that's where the dream ends.

By now, you've probably gotten the hang of moving back and forth between dreams and waking, and you know what's coming: the dreamer, in waking life, was stuck. This dreamer was working on a relationship pattern, and both the pattern, and what he needed to do to shift it, had become absolutely clear to him. He was on the one-yard line. His next step was to make a certain choice that would move this inner clarity to lived experience—the touchdown that would mean transformation. He doubted his ability to do it, though, and froze.

"Froze," in waking time, showed up in several ways, including this dreamer saying things like "yeahhhhh" while shaking his head no. What's interesting about this particular dream, though, is that it is showing that there is a whole other inner mental and emotional ground that is lined up and ready to succeed. While that can be really hard to see in waking time, it's easy to see in dream. And while the waking dreamer at first was transfixed on the frozen part of the dream, the Locating Aspect helped pull the view back to include the quarterback, the toss, and the one-yard line, expanding his way of looking at himself and the situation. Shifts like this give us the courage we need to take next steps—and hard choices—in our waking life.

To speak of dreams as having a Locating Aspect, an entrance or end, is in fact somewhat arbitrary because dreams are holistic; they are one complete image, like a painting. With a painting, I may start by focusing on a color in the upper right corner, then an image I see in the lower left, then go back up a bit to see what lies in the center. These are three separate views, but it's still one image. The same is true of our dreams. Even still, where I decide to start looking, where I end up, and what I focus on, tell me a lot about how I am choosing to approach things. They illustrate a particular point of view, and that helps me see things differently. When first looking at our dream, our waking focus usually locks in on one scene, like being "frozen." However, we can look around at other parts of the dream to bring additional perspectives into view. Then the entire experience changes.

The Locating Aspect is a perceptual ground that we can follow in a dream—we may start somewhere and go somewhere else, like from garden party to radical bad boy in an office. Sensing into each of these different locations, and what is happening within them, not only sets the stage of the action, it helps us understand it, especially when we seem to make strange choices in our dreams, which is where we head next.

The Presenting "I"

We just saw a dreamer get frozen in a dream thinking he can't catch the ball—he wants to, but doesn't think he can. But in the last chapter we saw a dreamer *actively* take a choice to walk away from relationship to stay with the sad part of the self in isolation. The football dreamer knew he was stuck in doubt. The red pepper dreamer, though, thought that walking away was a good decision. Both are the "I" in the dream. Let's take a closer look at this idea of the Presenting "I" and how we can put it to work for us, instead of being tricked by it.

Patterns, as we've discovered, have their own logic. Even more compelling, patterns spell relief. They seem to have worked before, so why not keep using them? Patterns function as a soothing Band-Aid on some unpleasant situation. We came up with this Band-Aid the first time as a legitimate attempt to resolve something. While it may not have been the best response, it was the best we could come up with in the moment; plus, we didn't die in the process. So, as far as the logical brain is concerned, it "worked."

The problem with patterns is not that we used them to begin with, but that we repeated them. Repetition stifles growth, but our dreaming self knows we can stretch. Patterns will show up in our dreams until we finally overcome them, and we can track them over the course of several dreams. A useful exercise is to leaf back through your dream journals from the past year or so and see if any patterns stick out. It's often easier to catch patterns over time than in the moment, and each new telling of it in a dream is giving us different angles so it becomes apparent to our waking eye. Here is an example of a pattern across two dreams, about two years apart, that also lets us discuss the Presenting "I".

First dream:

I am outside a convenience store trying to find a cup to get a soda. A man comes up in a car. He tells me to take the car. I don't know where to go, but I take the car anyway. I feel lost, and at one point I see the river and park the car. I get out and sit down and wait for someone to come and help me.

Second dream:

I am on a train heading to the city center. A girl I know gets on. She's wearing a bright yellow sweater and tells me she just got a new job. I see outside it is snowing, and get out, even though the stop is too early, and we aren't yet at the city center. The only things around are snowy fields, and an old airplane hangar where people are trying to get planes to fly but can't. I go in—maybe someone there can help me get to city center.

Did you catch the pattern? We can say it like this: when I don't know where I'm going in life, I stop and wait for someone to help me.

At first glance, this pattern doesn't seem so bad—why not wait until someone helps us? Dreams know we can help ourselves, though, and there are several elements in both dreams that show that the dreamer already has what they need to do exactly that.

In the first dream, an aspect of the dreamer shows up with a car. This is helpful energy, not unlike the football tossed by the quarterback in the first section. The car is movement, but the dreamer stops. That's the conflict. This is repeated in the second dream. The Locating Aspect is a train that is heading to the city center, which is not that different from a bull's-eye, or touchdown. The dreamer begins the dream directed and moving. The potential in this dream is the girl with the yellow sweater who just got a new job. The dreamer is heading in the *same direction* as this successful aspect. But then, abruptly, the dreamer gets off the train, i.e., stops. Snowy fields are present. The snowy fields represent a state of being that is not so different from being frozen, and are definitely contrasted with the sunny yellow of possibility the dreamer just separated from.

If the dreamer has a car, why park it? If they are heading to the bull's-eye of a real destination, why get off the train? We often ask ourselves similar questions in waking time—*why did I do that?*

Dreams are almost always experienced from the first-person point of view. This "I" drives the narration of the dream, directing the action, making the decisions, reacting to the scenarios, and experiencing the visceral, emotional elements of the dream. It is the perspective through which the dreamer is living their waking life at that moment. If that waking time is engaged in pattern, we see it in the dream. We can think of this as the currently activated state of the dreamer.

The other elements of the dream are also aspects of the dreamer. Because they are not the "I," they are the **active potential**: active, because out of all the many facets we could pull from in ourselves, the select ones that show up in the dream are those we have developed enough that they have emerged in form and become present to us. We can literally see them, so as energies they are vibrating quite strongly. They remain as just potential, though, because they aren't being used yet in waking life.

Knowing this about dreaming, we can look at our dreams consciously and consider the different perspectives as we work with them. In waking, we can ask ourselves why we got off the train, and we can get curious about the yellow sweater/new job aspect. Just that exercise will open up new options and help us to make tangible the active potentials we see. It sounds easy, but the challenge is remaining open to what our dreams are offering.

We are so much more than we allow ourselves to be—both individually and societally. All possibilities are available to us. We construct the world we live in by choosing what, of those limitless possibilities, we allow ourselves to see and then make tangible. Our seeing is limited by our belief systems. Like the footballer who doubts his ability to catch, and so does not. Dreaming saves us by enlarging our imagination. When we see the image of a perfect toss, the one-yard line, we are invited back to the place of limitless possibility. In our own lives we all have the ability to repair a relationship, act courageously, solve a problem, heal an emotional wound, and give and receive love. As a society, peace is possible. These aren't distant, elusive things to track down—they are present possibilities. The first step to making them tangible, though, is to open to seeing it as possible in the first place.

The Presenting "I" of the dream is the waking time, often narrowed, perspective that we bring into a dream. It is the orientation the dreamer thinks of as "me." "Me" is muscular, because it has agency, and we identify with it. Its point of view is familiar. When it makes a decision, it feels like it's doing the right thing. If we aren't careful when we wake up, and if the dream isn't immediately clear, we can stay "me." If we do that, we will tend to side with its point of view and block ourselves from exploring the other elements in the dream.

Let's look at an example:

> *I'm backstage at a big event. A world leader is about to announce me to come on stage to talk about my new project. There are some children back there with me. I think a bomb is going to go off, and I am worried about the children. I think to round them up and move us outside.*

This dream has a sense of impending disaster, specifically a bomb. Rounding up the children and moving them safely outside seems like the most logical thing to do. The dream ends before the action happens, though. I asked the dreamer what they wanted to do to resolve the dream, and they felt they needed to complete the action, finish rounding up the kids, and get them outside. They felt relief thinking about this option. However, in a very real sense this option would only increase their waking anxiety. How?

This dream gives us a big clue: "*I think* there will be a bomb." We don't ever actually see the bomb. If there were a bomb, we could find and disarm it without having to step out of the big event of talking about the new project. Therein lies the belief system: *if I step in the spotlight—reveal myself to others—I will bomb.* The pattern is how this belief system is reacted to, which is stepping out instead of stepping (in) onstage. If the dreamer had followed the resolve she wished, the relief would be a temporary sense of escaping (the perception of) the bomb. In other words, "if I never try, I never fail." The comfort that pattern offers is avoiding the uncomfortable stretch into the role of leader and speaking about, i.e., launching, the project.

Notice how much dreams help us understand their message by using common phrases and highlighting them with extra emotional intensity and situations to make sure we get it. "I'm going to bomb" is a common phrase relating to a speech or project absolutely failing. By putting that idea as a physical bomb in a situation, the dream makes it explicit for us. We can literally *see* the belief in a scenario. By doing so we can grasp it, take it in hand, and shift it.

The Locating Aspect of this dream is being backstage, but it is also the imminent invitation to speak on a stage to a waiting audience ready to listen. In waking life, there was, in fact, a project. If the dreamer had stayed in the Presenting "I" and chosen not to bring it to the public, the perceived disaster may have been averted, which may feel like relief. However, the urgings of the creative self that seek to be expressed would have persisted, generating increasing inner conflict.

Further, the pattern of avoiding takes the imaginative creative aspects of the Self—seen here as the children—even further away from the conscious grasp of the waking self. If this happens, it just ensures that the expression of the creative self that is currently back(stage) would remain out(side), hidden from others. Until the bomb of the belief system itself is faced, it will always be ticking somewhere. The dreamer would continue to sense this, feeling that any step onto the stage of their waking life could threaten to set it off.

Thinking about the Presenting "I" and pulling back the focus to include the other aspects of the dream, the world leader onstage comes into view. The world leader is also the dreamer. So are the children. Rather than moving the self and children out, both could come forward to meet the leader. When I reflected back the choices presented in the dream, the dreamer saw it from a different perspective. Rather than stepping out, as the Presenting "I" had thought, the now-engaged, awakened dreamer saw that stepping in and onstage became the solution.

In waking time, figuring out if we're acting from pattern can be challenging. We often make goals, and put great effort toward achieving them, only to realize later that it wasn't exactly the direction our true passion wanted us to take. Goals often masquerade as the "relief" of maintaining a restricted belief system, like not bringing forward a project for fear it will bomb and deciding on a different career path instead, or doubling down on your career because you doubt your ability to have a successful relationship. As humans, we like goals and the little markers of success we meet along the way. We tend to get so invested in them, though, that we forget to stop and ask ourselves if we're still heading in the right direction. Dreams help us do the work of discerning whether our Presenting "I" is aligned with our true self, or if other ideas are worth considering. We can also bring this idea of looking at ourselves through multiple perspectives into an active exercise for our waking life.

All the dreams we've looked at in respect to the Presenting "I" have been Clear Dreams. Clear Dreams present choice: they depict both block and potential. It's only Clear Dreams, with multiple perspectives, that will have a Presenting "I"—the "I" exists in contrast to the other perspectives, or perhaps mirroring them in some way. By contrast, Nightmares focus on emotional constriction, and Busy Dreams are made of piled-on emotional layers that contain no real agency. With Resolved Dreams our many perspectives are fully aligned.

Clear Dreams meet us at a moment when arresting emotions are no longer dominating our inner life, and we can raise our eyes to look out to bigger horizons. Meeting those horizons will require discovering the parts of the Self that have been hidden (the aspect of the Self who is invited onstage to present), diminished (the aspect able to catch the ball), suppressed (the aspect able to go all the way to the city center), or ignored (the aspect of the Self that is capable of true partnership). These parts show up as different aspects in Clear Dreams, but they also show up in our waking life when our waking life is in a Clear Dream state.

One of the ways we identify potential in a Clear Dream is by a bright color. Think back to the garden party dream and the woman with the yellow umbrella. That bright yellow gets our attention. It *feels* sunny. It's even round like the sun, and evokes the shining, relaxed sense of sitting by a pool. If we sense into that, our bodies are in a state of expansion. This is the state we are in when we are acting in our lives from a place of fluidity, curiosity, flow, and true self-expression. The woman under the yellow umbrella even has water in her pool, which highlights this sense of flow and fluidity. We know these moments of fluid expansion in waking life because they are the moments when we are fully engaged in what we are doing and life feels dynamic and vibrant.

Now let's contrast that to the Presenting "I" in this dream that is standing in a dry lap pool. Pools are meant to have water in them, so already we know something is missing. Lap pools are for going back and forth and there's nothing that points to pattern more strongly than that—no forward movement, repetitive, and eventually very boring. It is also a narrow rectangle, which, when sensed into, is the state of constriction the body feels when stuck in pattern. Any of these characterizations will show up in our waking time self-talk and conversations with others ("I'm not getting anywhere," "Every day is just the same old thing, over and over," "Life is dull"). If you catch yourself saying something like that again and again over a period of time, put on your detective hat and look at where your waking life is dull, and then search out where there is color. That color may be actual color, or the *feeling* of sunny, bright yellow; vibrant new green; reflective blue; and so on. In other words, the moments where there is a bright spot in your day, you feel your curiosity piqued or feel yourself expansive and engaged with something. What are you doing when you find it? Once you identify that, then notice what changes when you start to explore it.

This waking life activity points to another principle we can use when working with dreams: Find the Good and Grow the Good.[2] We tend, like the football dreamer, to latch on to the negative aspects of the dream and ignore the rest. In psychology terms, this is called the tendency toward negative valence, which means that we weigh negative events, information, and emotions more strongly than positive ones.[3] Finding the good involves training the eye and ear to be attentive to the jewel of possibility.

We can start that training in working with our night dreams. As an exercise, take your journal and look through a dream with the specific focus of finding the good, or the possibility present, in the dream. This often creates a shift in understanding the part of the dream that is pointing to what's possible, and where to go next. The same exercise can be applied in waking time to scenarios like stalemates with partners, dead ends with work teams, or seemingly irreconcilable differences between co-workers. Find what's possible and, instead of putting energy toward the difficulty, put energy towards growing the possibility. You'll find this moves almost any dead-end situation forward.

For most of us, our Big Question is to know who we are and what we are supposed to be doing in life. "*Where* am I?" is a more appropriate question than "*Who* am I?" because the Self is always in development. "*Who am I?*" connotes something static and fixed, like something we can finally know, once and for all, and stick with. If we check in, instead, to *where* we are in a certain moment or chapter in our lives—our current perspective—then we allow ourselves to be free in our movements. Then our "who" becomes more fluid and sets us up for bringing more aspects of the Self into realization. This broadens the waking choices that will become available in our lives. The more we grow, the more we are given chances to do so.

It is said that all dreams are one-sixtieth prophecy.[4] One way of understanding this is that dreams show us what is possible, but whether that ever comes to pass is up to us. That same source reminds us that all dreams contain an element of the absurd. To the stubborn view of the Presenting "I", breaking a pattern to stretch toward selfhood *is* absurd; pattern is safe, selfhood is mystery. To the person who thinks career is a safe harbor for a bruised heart, opening up to a relationship seems crazy. For the person who's extra eager to be in a relationship, the first bad boy that comes along seems much better than waiting for a real partner. Because the awake dreamer is the ultimate decider, no dream can be purely prophetic. We are the wild card that either chooses to make a possibility come to fruition or not.

This chapter looked at two different lenses for sifting through dreams, the Locating Aspect and the Presenting "I". Both help to orient us to our present tense. The Presenting "I" particularly helps us to identify latent potentials that we can activate in our waking lives. The next chapter looks specifically at ways to work with your dreams and to unlock the energy in your body that will help you to do so.

CHAPTER SEVEN

Conquering Blocks Through Dreams

"It's the end of the world. There is no more oxygen. I am standing on a frozen lake. Everything is frozen. I look and see that underneath the ice there is a little light. I look closer and see it is lit—somehow, under the ice, there is a candle burning. I kneel down and find I can breathe there. If I just cup my hands over the light and put my mouth there, I can breathe."

—DREAMER

A quarterback throwing a perfect pass, and the receiver freezing instead of catching it; a train heading to city center, and a dreamer stepping off before he gets there. In the last chapter we looked at dreams that contain both block and potential. The simple recognition of each begins to shift our experience. But we can go even further in our self-transformation by grappling with the block itself. When we do that, we take charge of our experience and consciously move our life in a new direction. This chapter returns to the idea of Unresolved Dreams and Necessities and teaches you how to do a waking dream exercise to address the Necessities of your dreams and transform them from unresolved to resolved.

The Origin of Block

We've looked at a number of dreams so far, most of them night dreams, but some of them generated by an imagery exercise while awake, like the woman in Chapter Two who saw the tree with the golden almond that was blocked by the cardboard box. If you remember, that entire chapter looked at how the image we have in our mind's eye is our blueprint for action. The cardboard box between the woman and the golden almond was the image of the mental block that was keeping her from making a decision and moving forward in her life.

Our inner images are forms given to the energies in our body. Energy itself is not tangible, yet it moves us tangibly, most notably in the emotions and feelings we experience that cause us to tremble, constrict, open up, and so on. Images give us a visual to better grasp what is happening. The emotions, feelings, and physical characterizations will show themselves in some way in the specific details of the image.

Energies express themselves through our physical, emotional, mental, and spiritual planes. When we are balanced, our body's energy flows fluidly. If we have a block, like the cardboard box, not only is the block affecting our actions, it is also tying up our energy in some way; instead of flowing through these four planes fluidly, the energy gets stuck.

We can think of how this works by comparing it to having a cast on our arm. The body functions, but there is the block of the cast on one part of ourselves. We can still do things, but our range of motion and the dexterity with which we perform are diminished. Because of that limitation, we then choose limited movements that don't require much use of the arm at all. Maybe we even decide to sit activities out altogether, because the effort of trying to do something with the cumbersome cast is too much.

This may include missing a social event. We may even start to feel sorry for ourselves. One little block ends up restricting the entire scope of how we live and feel, in all areas of life.

The binding-up of energy into a block requires energy for us to maintain it. We also looked at that earlier when I challenged you on page 67 to flex a muscle and hold it. The amount of energy required of us to sustain a block means that we start to allocate a tremendous amount of inner resources to maintain something that is actually stopping us from advancing our lives. Our normally fluid movement of energy is diverted to the block, draining us of its full use in other areas. Change the block, though, and that energy releases.

If you think back to many of the dreams we've looked at, an overall pattern emerges of our inner energetic system flowing until it is disrupted by the waking, thinking self that halts it. Warm-hearted Jake traveling, and a dreamer staying behind; dancing with a dancer who moves perfectly, and the dreamer stepping out; the woman heading towards a golden almond but circling in place because a cardboard box was in the way. In all these cases there is movement that is halted or stopped in some way.

Stopping natural movement is counter to a balanced, embodied state. Everything alive in the world is in constant movement—our planet turns on its axis and rotates around the sun; oceans wax and wane with the tides; our bodies are ever-breathing, the heart always beating. *Stop*, in nature, means stagnation, which signals disease. If you've ever been hiking and stumbled across a murky swamp you get a clear idea of how different that motionless, dark, dank, smelly water is compared to a crystal blue, running, bubbling stream.

The key to shifting from stagnant to active—from murky swamp to running stream—is to return to the block that is holding us up. That block is accessible via image. The image is the interface between body, mind, and energy (which includes emotions and feelings). To shift the block, we turn our attention to, and interact directly with, the image itself, just as I prompted the woman to engage with the cardboard box and find a way over, under, through, or around it.

Because we are so habituated to leaning on our logical, rational mind, we tend to think that interacting with block and image means *thinking about* it. We start ascribing theory to the block; we wonder why it's a cardboard box in our way instead of something else, or we give ourselves abstracted assignments such as "I need to be bolder in making choices in my life." But the woman who saw that cardboard box between her and the golden almond wasn't lacking boldness. As I reported in that chapter, as soon as she left our session, she signed a lease and in three months was operating at capacity and hiring associates.

Acting on, instead of *thinking about*, is how we change. *Thinking about* uses the same cognitive processing system that generated the problem in the first place, as we saw in the last chapter on patterns. If we stay in the logical-rational mode of thinking, we'll go around and around, but never forward. *Acting on* returns us to the dynamic and responsive neurobiological system that is developmentally generative.

Image is our origin of action. When we see block as an image, it's the *image* that we must work with literally, as a physical thing, not as a concept.

Let's explore what that looks like.

Block and Necessity

Blocks in dreams are easy to find. When we sense into the dream, the conflicts we bump against reverberate with physical sensations and emotional reactions. These visceral sensations and emotional reactions are signposts, pointing us directly to the block.

Look again at the dream at the top of the chapter. The description is frozen, still, iced over, without oxygen. The visceral experience of the body is to feel restricted, cold, suffocating. The dreamer feels and says *it's the end of the world*. We physically sense the block and can state it verbally: "frozen" (no movement), "can't breathe" (restriction/no oxygen).

As soon as we locate the block, there arises in us automatically a yearning for something different; no one wants to stay frozen and restricted. The restriction in this dream makes us want to move and release from the restriction so we can breathe a little.

From freezing to moving; from restriction to having space enough to breathe. We've identified the block and what needs to happen instead. This is the first step in changing the dream. Now we have to find the one change that will bring about that shift.

With this end-of-the-world dream, we see that the emotional, thinking self really feels stuck. Frozen, specifically. And not just frozen like the footballer who doesn't reach for the pass, here the entire landscape is literally iced over. For the body, the dire circumstance is not whatever is happening in waking time—whether the challenge is at work or home, or what the details are—so much as that the dreamer has frozen all their energies and is *no longer actively working to resolve it*. The glowing life-force potential that the dreamer could use to respond, however, is always present. The dreamer sees it in this dream as the candle; and, seeing it, it gets the dreamer moving again: *I look. . . there is a little light. . . I look closer. . . there is a candle burning there. . . I kneel down and find I can breathe there.* The light is the key to breaking up the frozenness and restriction and allowing movement and breath to return.

In Chapter Four, I introduced you to a concept called the Necessity of the dream. The Necessity is the one change that will shift all the conflicts in the dream. There may be many things wrong in the dream—a frozen landscape, a lack of oxygen, a sense of the end of the world. There is, however, only one Necessity. It is the linchpin on which all the many conflicts are tied. When we identify and respond to the Necessity, all the other conflicts will shift, the Unresolved Dream will become resolved, and our body-energy will return to balance.

In the end-of-the-world dream, we can put it together like this: The block is the state of being frozen and restricted, with the consequence being no oxygen. What we want, instead, is movement, which will give the ability to breathe. Now we ask ourselves how to achieve that aim, which will be the Necessity. The key is the light from the candle that is burning somehow under the ice, generating oxygen. The Necessity, then, is to free the candle from under the ice. If we can free the candle, which is the energy-potential, then we reverse the situation of frozen, and return the dreamer to movement (breathing) and the body to balance (Resolved Dream).

Now that we've figured this out in our minds, we have to really do it.

Shifting Block with the Waking Dream Exercise

In Chapter Two, in the session with the woman and the golden almond, I recount giving her a short imagery exercise to return to the image and address the Necessity. This short imagery exercise is called a Waking Dream exercise. We use it to engage directly with dreams to transform blocks. Here's how it goes:

First make sure you are in a quiet location where you won't be disturbed. Sit comfortably, either in lotus pose or in a chair with your back straight and arms and legs uncrossed. These two postures allow for the free movement of energy in our body. Close your eyes, and breathe out three times. On the first exhale see the number three. Exhale again seeing the number two. Then exhale, seeing the number one. See the number one tall, clear, and very bright. Then, see that you reenter the dream and address the Necessity, staying in response to new images that arise. Continue to breathe throughout the exercise. When it's done—and you'll know it is because everything will shift, and both the dream and your physical body will *feel* balanced—breathe out again and open your eyes.

The Necessity in the end-of-the-world dream was to free the candle from under the ice. *How* that happens is up to you and your spontaneous imagination.

Returning to the dream while awake puts us directly in contact with our spontaneous imagination where images are produced. I say spontaneous because they are different from *deciding* to see something, like a yellow chair. The images of the spontaneous imagination are not ones we forcefully conjure. While we may enter a dream knowing we have to free the candle from under the ice and go in with an icepick to do it, the moment we engage with the image, it will spontaneously shift in response, and in surprising ways.

Our bodies are in constant relationship with us, providing feedback in every moment. If you put your finger on your arm, both finger and arm will warm up. Blood will start flowing from both directions toward each other. Similarly, when we turn our conscious attention to the images of our body, the images will respond.

To enter the feedback dialogue, though, we have to consciously engage with it—directing finger to arm, or attention to inner images. It is the conscious, waking mind that stepped out of the feedback dialogue to halt the body's natural energetic flow and lock it in pattern. Redirecting our conscious attention to dialogue with the spontaneous inner images reengages our natural movement.

This may seem a bit abstract at first, because as adults we spend so much time in our logical processes that we may not even realize we have inner images, other than those in our dreams. Try this: the next time you have a little challenge, like receiving a new, irritating work assignment, pay attention to the metaphor that springs to mind about how that makes you feel. I've had clients say things like "a lion locked in a cage," "trapped under a pile of rocks," or "pushing a boulder uphill." Usually this is directly describing the inner image, and if you close your eyes, you will likely see that very image. (Which means, by the way, that you can shift it!)

The images of our spontaneous imagination emerge from the same default network neural processing system as does our night dreaming, allowing us to imagine beyond block and pattern. The free flow of new information in dreams is something we passively receive. By doing the Waking Dream exercise, we intentionally couple our active conscious attention with the default network. This coupling dynamizes the change by partnering conscious will and imaginative possibility.

Working in the spontaneous imagination in a Waking Dream exercise entails letting images arise as they do in dreaming. Trust the body's intelligence and stay in the imaginative space, as opposed to a fantasy or what you wish would happen. As the images shift, stay in response to them, knowing that you have all the tools in your imagination to do so.

So, how did the end-of-the-world dreamer free the candle? The dreamer went into the Waking Dream exercise with only the aim to free it, and no idea yet how they would do so. Once there, immediately their imagination called up a Russian icebreaker, those ships that have huge "jaws" on the front that tear through icebergs to clear shipping lanes. It surprised both me and the dreamer, and it showed us the huge amount of creative energy this dreamer contains. An entire frozen landscape is big, just as a Russian icebreaker is gigantic. Rather than chip away at the candle, the body dealt with it full-on. That surprise of the unusual icebreaker, and what it conveys as a muscular, powerful energy, tells us about the capacity of our spontaneous imagination when we allow it to work freely. If you stay in the imaginative space, you will not only resolve the block, you will surprise yourself by jetting to a whole new place in your inner evolution. Instead of a lateral shift of A to B, you'll jump to a completely new experience.

Interacting with image is simple. When we start doing it, however, it seems strange. Can shifting an image really change anything? The desire to figure out the circumstance causing the block—the thing in waking life that made the landscape frozen, for example—is strong because the logical-rational mind wants everything to make sense on its very narrow terms. But it is exactly because we are working with a different part of the body-mind that we are able to transform those blocks.

The block is image, not a thought or theory. Because image is our blueprint for action, changing a blocked image means that our waking experience will change. Even without picking apart the circumstances of the old conflict, our changed inner situation will cause us to approach the outer situation in a new way. That new way will utilize all our creative resources and, therefore, will be automatically different. That difference cracks open a world of possibility. It changes everything.

In the end-of-the-world Waking Dream exercise, as soon as the Russian icebreaker arrived, the entire scene immediately and spontaneously became a flourishing, verdant meadow with wildflowers of many different colors. Plenty of sun, growth everywhere, and the previously frozen aspects now wild and colorful. The dreamer did not wish for this scene or have it in mind beforehand—it simply appeared. It is the image of the energy of the block once it has been released from frozen to movement.

The embodied aspect of the experience is critical. We physically feel a shift from block to resolve (icy frozen to sunny meadow). Physical sensation is what our body understands as real. By contrast, thinking remains disembodied, even abstract. With thinking we can *consider* different solutions, but they remain "just thoughts." Physically *feeling* a shift from block to resolve, however, means that the resolve is registered as an actual experience. It becomes a new set-point in the body-mind.

Those same physical sensations carry with them an inner knowing about how we perceive our present experience, as well as how to resolve the waking block. That inner knowing can't be accessed while in a frozen state of being. It can, however, be found when in a sunny meadow state of being.

When in front of a problem, the challenge is never that we don't know what to do, it's that the part of ourselves that does know, or can figure it out, is tied up in the block. Deep down we have a pretty good idea what is challenging us and what we need to do to overcome the challenge. Generally, it's all the thinking that gets in our way of doing it. Getting out of thinking and back to image connects us right away to the waking scenario. The exercise of identifying the block in image, and the experience of responding to it, connects the dots for what is possible, and returns our energy to do what it takes to make change in our waking life.

In the next section, we'll practice with a few dream scenarios so that you get the hang of finding and addressing Necessities.

Practice with Necessities

There is a little trick that can help in finding the Necessity, which is the idea that everything contains its opposite—hot/cold, night/day. By reversing from one to the other we change the situation. If something is too hot, for example, we can address it by bringing in something cool; if something is too dark, we can bring in light.

One way to think of this is to consider balance as home base. Getting off balance means I've strayed off home base in one direction or another. To get back, I need to reverse that direction and return home.

Finding Necessities in Nightmares is fairly easy, because Nightmares generally present one simple scenario. Probably the most common Nightmare (if I had a dollar for every time I've heard it. . .) is this:

I'm in a bathroom, in front of a toilet that is full to the edge with excrement—it's going to overflow!

The block is, literally, the blocked toilet. The Necessity is to flush it. That's it!

We could ascribe all kinds of theories to the blocked toilet: things we need to let go of that are backed up or overloaded, too many commitments. . . All we need to do, though, is flush the toilet in this scenario. The more we talk about it, the longer we would be standing in front of it! No one wants to do that.

Nightmares can trick us out of dealing with them, though, because of their emotional intensity. Here's an example:

I'm standing outside of a dark room, and I'm terrified to enter! It's so dark, and I don't know what's in there!

Some dreamers might think the Necessity is to go somewhere else, away from the dark room; after all, that would get rid of the terror of the dream. However, the other thing we have to remember when working with Necessities is what we learned in the last chapter about the Presenting "I". That "I" may be too afraid to face the Nightmare—fear is what generates the Nightmare in the first place—but the dreaming self knows better. Addressing a Necessity will always involve stretching ourselves a little bit.

In this dream, standing outside is reversed by going in, even though—and especially because—it terrifies us to do so. The difference in the Waking Dream exercise, versus the Nightmare experience, is that the dreamer returns consciously, with access to their inner toolbox. If the dark is terrifying, the dreamer can enter with a flashlight or turn on the light. A light reverses the situation of too dark. Whatever is seen in the room with the light on will always be something we can work with.

We see this need to stretch ourselves in this excerpt from a Clear Dream:

> *I am in a hotel. It's summer—warm and sunny outside. I see buildings at the opposite side of the street. I wear a red dress. I'm with my family, including my two little nieces. Someone will come to take the girls and us—I don't feel good about it. There are no bathrooms in this hotel, because they want to make us move outside. Suddenly a man in a Spider-Man costume stands next to me. We are close to the window. He wants to fly out. He says we will see each other on the other side of the street. I say, "Don't you see that I'm not in a costume and I don't have the superpower to fly?" He disappears.*

The dream goes on, but we don't need the rest to know what needs to happen. Start with sensing into the dream: summer, warm, and sunny outside. "I" am, however, inside. Who wants to stay inside when outside is nice and sunny? All the focus is outside and on the superhero's desire to go to the other side of the street. Everything in the dream—the hotel, Spider-Man—is trying to get the dreamer outside, but the "I" doesn't feel good about it and doesn't think they can. We know full well, however, that the "I" is capable.

The possibility in this Clear Dream is the color that pops out: red. Both the dreamer, the "I," and Spider-Man are in red. Spider-Man has superpowers to get outside and to the opposite side of the street.

The opposite side represents the opposite of the restrictive POV that the "I" is currently holding. Sensing into the color red, it is a really vibrant and active color. It's telling us that the superpower of Spider-Man is something the dreamer also has, even though the Presenting "I" doesn't get it. *She is literally wearing the superhero costume she denies having.*

This dream already lays out for us the block and reverse: inside/outside, this side of the street/opposite side of the street. The Necessity is to get outside. Unlike a Nightmare, this Clear Dream comes with a ready help: Spider-Man. He can be summoned in a Waking Dream to get the "I" out the window and over to the other side of the street—or wherever else the spontaneous imagination may take them.

Clear Dreams may have more details, scenes, and nuances than Nightmares, but by both sensing into what does (or doesn't) feel balanced and by working with the idea of reversing, we get to their core. Here's one last example for us to look at:

> *I am in Dad's home. He has a large white room with high ceilings. The room feels expansive, spacious, and complete. There is a group of kids all wearing sweaters of the different colors of the rainbow. Inside the room they are playing baseball. At first, they are playing directly in front of where the giant mirror on the wall is. I can sense that the ball will hit the mirror and will shatter it. I get the kids to move over and play in front of a big painting instead.*

At first glance, this dream seems resolved. The space is clean, the ceilings are high, and it feels expansive. But again, we have a situation of color, movement, and play stuck inside. It's close, but not quite right. If we sense into it, there's something stifling about it—the kids are restrained in their play and made to stay in one confined area. When I sense this, I want to break out, and so do the kids, which is what shattering the mirror is all about.

This dream is particularly fun because it sets opposites in a bit of a pun. The Locating Aspect of this dream is in Dad's home. The game the kids want to break out and play is baseball, which has a different kind of home: home plate. As a dreamer, the colorful, imaginative, creative energies aren't able to fully express themselves under Dad's roof. It's not a bad place to be, per se, but it's not a place of free, independent movement. Each of us seeks to be our own person, bringing our own uniqueness to the world. In this dream there is a mirror, which reflects back. What is it reflecting? Things under Dad's roof. Rather than mirroring Dad, the creative aspects of this dreamer want to play in their own game, get to their own home plate.

The block is staying under Dad's roof, the resolve is to get out from under it. Specifically, the Necessity is to move dreamer and the colorful kids outside, which is exactly what this dreamer did in the Waking Dream exercise. Stepping out, the images shifted, and suddenly she was at the beach, with an expansive horizon, that she said felt like "the true me."

The dreamer in Dad's home was working for her father in waking life, running his business. She was doing well, her work was appreciated, and the family was "in a good place"—all the clean space we saw in the white room in the dream. The only problem was that she didn't want to do that anymore. As soon as we worked on the dream she said, "I need to break up with my dad." "Break up" is an interesting choice of phrase for several reasons, including the obvious connection to shattering the mirror. Breaking up the image of the "daughter that runs the father's company," going outside to play with the other possibilities life has to offer, and finding out who she is when her identity is independent from her father, is exactly what she did next, even moving to a new city to explore something completely different.

Finding Necessities in Waking Life

We can just as easily find Necessities in waking life. By now you've gotten into the practice of looking at waking scenarios as a dream: deciding what kind of dream they are, whether they are resolved or unresolved, and noticing patterns that appear. Now you can add to that practice looking for the block and finding the Necessity. Here's a waking life example from a client:

The client worked at a high-paying consulting job and complained that they felt overloaded, stressed, and unfulfilled. Their only outlet was flying to a weekend, sport-centered getaway that they crammed between Friday at 5:00 p.m. and Monday at 9:00 a.m., which left them exhausted rather than rested. After the completion of each project, the client felt "wrecked." In between consulting contracts, the client worked on a small business they'd started, which they called a side hustle and whose importance they downplayed. The "real job" made money; the small business was "just an idea" and didn't bring in income. However, I soon realized that when this client was working on their own business, they worked longer hours, more intensely, didn't take the weekend getaways, and were energized instead of exhausted. The problem was that, just as they got going on their own business, another consulting contract would come in. Then they would drop their own business, and take off, back on the road to being "wrecked."

This waking scenario is a Clear Dream; there is both block and potential. If it were a night dream, we would see the "wrecked" as some kind of tight situation and the possibility of their side business as the color. The trick here is naming the block. The client thought it was the demanding job and was trying to remedy that problem with the intense weekend getaways. This was just pattern, however; repeated incessantly, even though it was not working. When exploring the idea of the small business, they thought the block was "not enough money." We know better. The block is *the belief system that says the small business won't succeed*. That block had them running away from the small business each time it was just about to take off. Because it was never fully focused on, it never gained momentum and therefore, to the untrained eye, it didn't seem to offer anything much.

With this dream we get a full picture of what happens when we bind our energy into block. So much valuable creativity and drive was wasted on the consulting job that resulted in feeling "wrecked." By contrast, working on the passion project was additive. What we are talking about is abstract—we can't quantify energy in our body as we can the battery on our phone. From the client's view, the idea that, by harnessing and redirecting the energy that was currently squandered on the consulting job, she could power the small business to success was still theory and not compelling enough. The embodied experience of it, though, was.

I had my client sense, feel, and describe the physical sensations of the intensity of the consulting work, the intensity of the sporty getaways, and "wrecked" at the end of the cycle. This included naming any colors, sense impressions, and images that arose. Then I had her do the same for the feelings when working on the small business. "Wrecked," with all its brown colors, chest-tightening, stomach-clenching sensations couldn't hold up next to a sweeping, sun-bathed hillside planted with vegetables in the Mediterranean that was the small business. The small business view was expansive and exciting; the embodied experience speaks its truth, and that is what, ultimately, worked with this client. Her side business today? Full time and flourishing, like the vegetables in her image.

Somatically we understand unresolved and resolved, imbalance and balance. Just as listening to someone practice the piano, the wrong note is obvious. The contrast between the two becomes a call to make a choice.

In each of the cases in this book where we've taken a night dream and brought it back to waking life—from the car speeding toward the gaping hole to the woman who moves the colorful kids away from breaking the mirror—the dreamer knows immediately what they need to do to shift the dream to something they can manifest in their waking experience. The speeding car dreamer saw how impossible the work/travel schedule was; the woman knew she needed to "break up" with her dad. When imbalance appears in a dream, we are returned with a focused awareness to the uncomfortable physical experience of it. Then we are left with a clear question: *Which feeling is the experience I want to live*?

Suddenly knowing what we need to do after working with a dream, or a waking scenario as a dream, is not extraordinary—we usually *know* we shouldn't keep going at a crazy pace or stay in a job that isn't fulfilling. We don't arrive at these places haphazardly. Frequently, we face a challenge and have an emotional reaction to it—fear, resistance—and then begin to try and correct for the emotion, like the client going on intense, exhausting weekend getaways, rather than digging down to name the real problem. The work of finding the Necessity helps us to correct this time-consuming trap.

At the same time, we can also learn to use our dreams to manage our emotions and avoid the trap altogether, which is where we turn in the next chapter.

CHAPTER EIGHT

The Life Plan: Transforming Your Dreams in Waking Life

"I'm in a red rock canyon. The rocks are red.
The dirt is red, like the Australian or Sedona Desert.
I'm in the bottom of the canyon driving on a road
that has big red boulders on it everywhere.
Somehow my truck climbs over them.
The further I go, the narrower the canyon gets.
It's getting dark and I can't see as well.
Finally, I'm just boxed in."

—DREAMER

We often think of emotions as something that happens to us, beyond our control. "He made me so mad!" "That article was disturbing, I can't stop worrying about it." "They sold our company, I'm freaking out." In each of these cases, we put the source of emotion outside us; it's the other person, an article, or event that is at fault. It seems like these things consume us in some way, triggering a state of being that we can only submit to until it either "blows over," like a bad storm, or we can "release" it, like a bomb we've been put in charge of carrying that we can finally let go. Nothing could be further from the truth. Instead of something happening *to* us, emotions are an experience inside us, which means we can learn to control them.[1]

Emotions are an expression of energy—*our* energy. Their origin is our own body, not an outside entity or circumstance. This same energy forms our primary instincts, primary and secondary emotions, and feelings. Each of these are expressions of the rhythms of our unique, individual body, and the consequences of moving out of rhythm when we encounter a stimulus, negative or positive. Working with the rhythms, we can control the movement of energy to choose its appropriate "container"—like whether we want to experience compassion instead of anger.

This chapter presents the **Life Plan,**[2] a somatic map that details the movement of our base energy or life force. It presents a way of looking at the bodily basis of emotion and provides a tool to direct the energy of emotion to the expression of our choice. It is a staple of the dreaming work, because it visualizes and operationalizes many of the underlying principles of why we dream one thing or another.

I'll take you step-by-step through the Life Plan and provide charts to illustrate it. It's best, however, if you draw your own. I'll give you exercises to get you started, and through your dreaming practice you can continue to fill it in. Each of the seven kinds of dreams correspond to each of the aspects of the Life Plan, and we'll map them onto each other so that you have a complete tool for working with your dreams—night and day.

Where It All Starts—The Primary Instincts

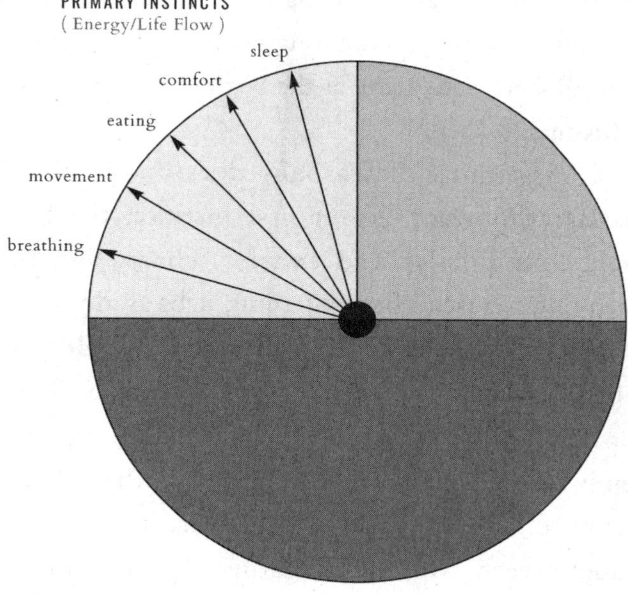

Figure 1

In utero we are basically a curled-up ball of extremely dense, concentrated energy. This is represented in Figure 1 as the black dot in the center of the drawing. This tight, dense ball of energy is our life force. It contains all the energy that we have been given for our life journey. Managing this finite energy through balancing our emotions and safeguarding our natural rhythms conserves health and prolongs life.[3] Like a nuclear reactor we can use our energy to power our life's activities; if poorly managed, however, it can explode, melt down, and cause chain reactions that affect a lot of people. Learning how to manage this incredible energy, then, is also our road to inner development and part of our life's work and responsibility.

In utero, this tight ball of energy is contained, a lot like an egg. As soon as we are born, though, this tight, contained energy is released; like hitting the "go" button, in the wide-open space of the outer world the energy starts flowing and coursing through the channel of our physical body, animating us. It moves in five specific ways, and they all start right away at the birth event. They are called our **Primary Instincts.**

What is the first thing that a baby does upon being born? Cry! This is **Breath**, which is our first instinct; the life force moves through our inhales and exhales, channeling through body, lungs, mouth, nose. The next thing a baby does is move. Arms and legs wave and stretch in all directions. **Movement** is the second primary instinct. This movement is also directed at searching for the breast. When a newborn is placed on the mother's abdomen it will wiggle on its own up the mother's belly until it finds sustenance.[4] That takes us to the third primary instinct, which is **Eating.** Breath, Movement, Eating: the first three Primary Instincts.

What comes next? Most people say excretion, but this is another form of eating—it is all part of the input/output of the nourishing process. Think again to what happens next with baby after eating: baby is held, wrapped in arms and blanket, warmed, and succored with words and song, kisses, touch, and stroking. This instinct is **Comfort.** With comfort, baby **Sleeps.** Comfort and Sleep are the fourth and fifth Primary Instincts.

The five primary instincts of Breath, Movement, Eating, Comfort, and Sleep are the *fundamental* expressions of our energy and therefore fundamental *needs* of the body. As needs, they are nonnegotiable.

The five primary instincts are shown on Figure 1 as arrows to depict the dynamic movement between them. Our life force energy expresses itself through these instincts like moving channels through which the energy flows. This flow moves in specific rhythms that are unique to each of us.[5] My natural rhythm of breathing is not yours, nor are the times and length my body likes to sleep. For some, the stimulation of light is exciting and energizing; others prefer the coziness of lower light. Some babies prefer to curl up and be bundled tight, others kick off blankets and stretch into starfish poses.

The flow of our life force is always moving, just like everything alive is in constant movement. The vibration of electrons, your heart beating, your lungs pumping—even your blood cells singing along the rush of fluid in your veins—are all visual traces of this energy.

So far so good. When the energy of our life force is allowed to flow unobstructed in its natural rhythms, then we are in the balanced state of homeostasis; everything is in its right place. It's a lot like water moving evenly through a garden hose; we are the hose, the water is our energy, and when it flows we feel centered. However, we don't always live in rhythm, do we? We skip meals, we get too little sleep, we hold our breath or pant when distressed. Disrupting our rhythms obstructs the flow of our life force energy—it kinks the hose. Now what?

From Instinct to Emotion

The life flow is energy, and energy can't be stopped. So if the hose gets kinked, the energy has to go *somewhere*. It has to keep moving, but if the channel of the primary instincts is blocked, the life force energy turns back in on itself and seeks another channel of expression. Just like kinking a hose, it backs up, concentrates, and forces another outlet. This brings us to Figure 2.

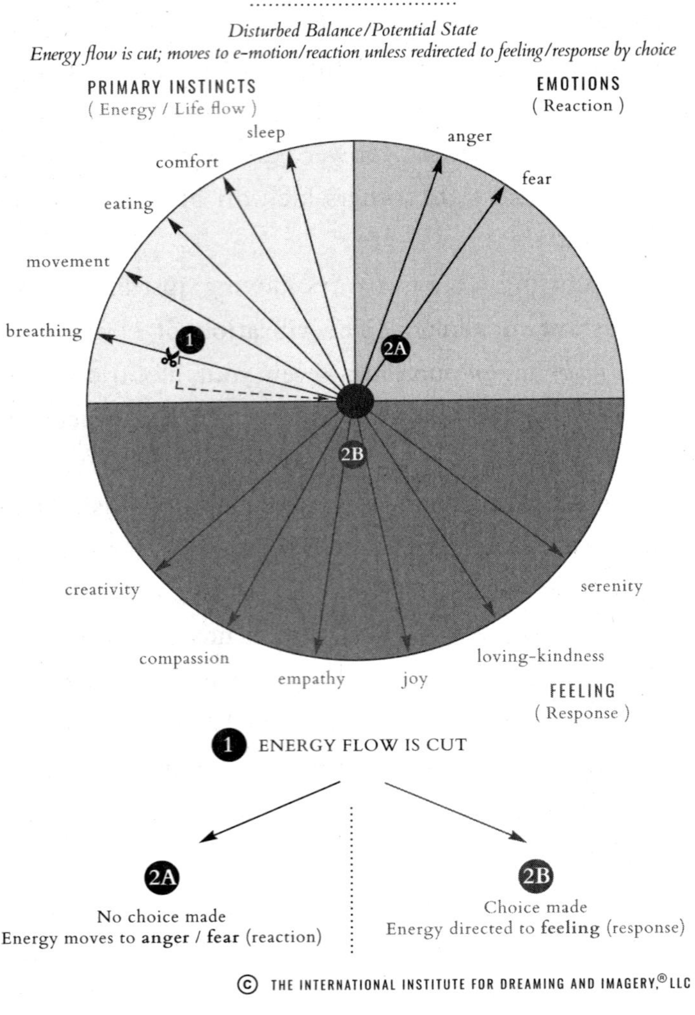

Figure 2

If we cut the natural flow of life force energy, it will find another way to move. That initial cut concentrates it—just like when we kink a garden hose and the water comes out with greater force when we first let go, before settling back into normal flow. The concentrated energy of our life force moves through our body in one of two different expressions that we recognize and name as **anger** or **fear**.

Anger and fear are the two **Primary Emotions**, and they are characterized by intense physical movement. We may ball our fists, flex our biceps, and prepare to punch, which we will call anger; or, we may step back or run and call it fear. You may be used to thinking of this as fight or flight. This concentrated energy can serve a purpose and help us deal with challenges. If we imagine ourselves as a caveman encountering a grizzly bear, that concentrated energy will help us to either fight and overcome the bear, or run from it and save our lives. Either of those two actions will disperse the intensity of the concentrated energy, and the life force will return to the natural, rhythmic flow.

There's a little problem, though. The bears we stumble upon in our modern, daily life are pugnacious family members, demanding bosses, and other such threats. To our body it is no different. We still hold our breath, tighten movements, and concentrate our energy. We can't really fight or run in these instances, though. This means we cut the flow of life force energy a second time, kinking the hose on *both* ends. Now what?

Notice on Figure 2 that cutting the flow of life force energy from any of the five primary instincts puts us in a state of disturbed balance. In that very instance of being cut, we are no longer in a state of homeostasis. At the same time, in that immediate instance of being cut, before the energy expresses itself in another way, it is also a potential state. There is a tiny little window—maybe a second or two—where the energy gathers itself before heading in a new direction. The *first* place it wants to go, and where it will go if we do nothing, is to anger or fear. But it doesn't have to. If we catch that window, we can redirect the energy somewhere else, to a place of feeling. This happens when we intervene consciously through choice. We can use the concentrated energy in the imbalanced state to fuel that conscious redirection. Energy going to anger or fear is a *reaction*; directing the energy to feeling, instead, is a *response*. When we respond and direct our energy to feeling, we return to our natural rhythms.

Feeling, to which we give words like compassion, courage, peace, and joy, is synonymous with homeostasis. You may be asking, *Can we really shift from anger to joy in an instant?* Remember we're talking about energy. What we call anger or fear is just one way in which energy flows; likewise, what we call joy (or courage or compassion) is a different characterization of the flow of energy. The energy in both cases is the same. To return to the garden hose image, our physical body is the hose, the water is the energy. But it is our conscious mind that is *holding* the hose, and we can aim it wherever we want.

From Primary Emotions to Secondary Emotions and Substitute Needs

Let's bring this abstract conversation home with an example. Imagine being a child playing happily with a toy. From behind, a sibling suddenly runs up and kicks the toy. What happens? The answer is not "I get mad." The answer is, we suddenly suck in our breath at the surprise. Energy, expressed before through the primary instinct of breathing, is now stopped. It has to move, however, and so it heads toward an expression that allows it to do so—we cock our fists and prepare to whack our sibling.

From the perspective of our life force energy, whacking our sibling is a good idea. If we do it, the concentrated energy that takes the form of our tensed muscles is released with the punch, much like pummeling the grizzly bear. From the perspective of our mother, however, it's a bad idea. Just as we pull our arm back to let it fly, she yells at us to knock it off. Now we stop the energy a second time. What happens to it in our body?

When the breathing was cut, energy found a movement through anger, but before it can express and disperse, it is cut again. Now it again turns back in on itself and stagnates. Very much like our garden hose example, now kinked on both ends, it bulges out and hardens[6]; the concentrated energy that would have moved through anger or fear becomes dense. This is a fully disbalanced state and brings us to Figure 3 below and on the next page.

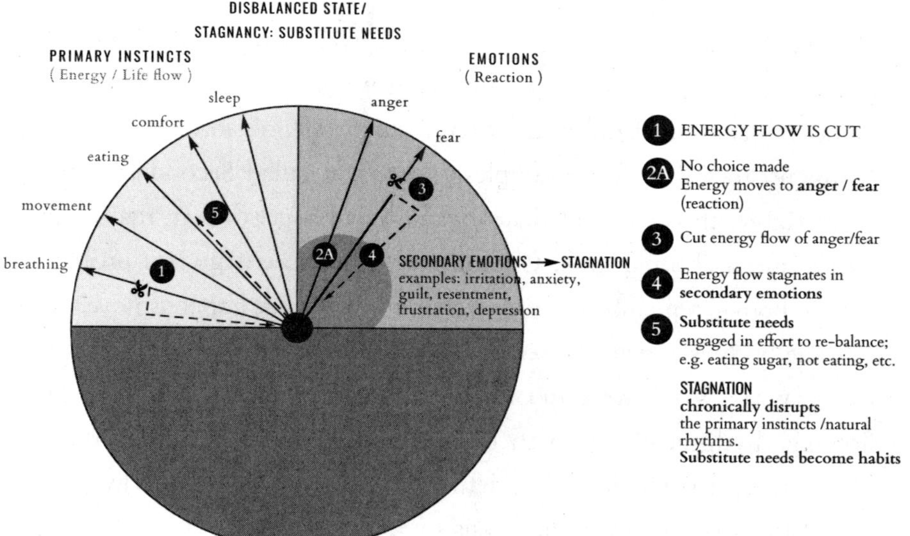

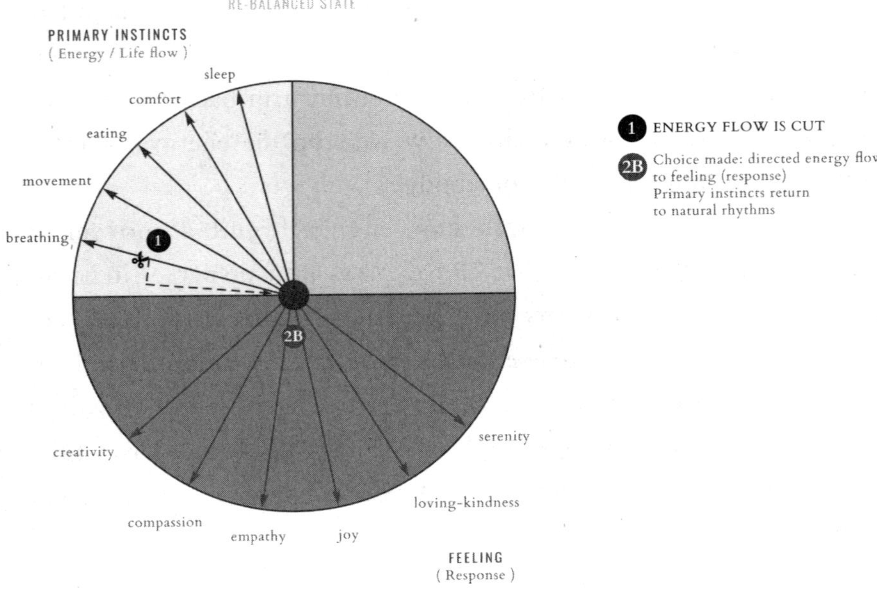

Figure 3

The stagnant energy that was blocked from moving through either anger or fear expresses itself in numerous ways that we experience and name as persistent irritation, worry, anxiety, depression, guilt, or resentment, to give a few examples. These are called **Secondary Emotions.** Rather than the immediate experience of anger or fear, the energy settles into a chronic state. Chronic, or stagnant, energy is a problem for the body—remember, energy *has* to move. What happens now?

The body is constantly seeking homeostasis; this is a physical law, like gravity. When we don't allow it the preferred choice of energy flowing rhythmically through its natural channels, it finds a forced outlet. It *has* to. The forced outlet is some means to keep energy moving and try to achieve homeostasis by a work-around. If breathing is halted from its natural rhythm, for example, that forced outlet might be smoking, or addictive exercise. The work-around for breathing, or any of the other blocked primary instincts, might be online shopping, masturbation, or compulsively eating sugary snacks.[7] I gained fourteen pounds writing my PhD dissertation—unfortunately I didn't do a very good job of working my own Life Plan, and twelve hours a day in front of the computer turned into too many trips to the freezer for coconut ice cream (with chocolate chips, of course).

The forced outlet that our body finds is called a **Substitute Need.** Giving in to substitute needs doesn't return us to a natural rhythm. They are only a slapped-on bandage for the body desperately seeking equilibrium. Using our kinked garden hose example, a substitute need would be like a small fissure somewhere; there is a slight release of pressure through this little crack, but the hose remains contorted and the flow is fundamentally blocked. Because of this, substitute needs become habits.

It wasn't my first bowl of ice cream that posed a problem; it was that I ate a bowl of it every day during the summer of my most intense writing. Eating ice cream, running, shopping—none of these are problems if they are in balanced proportion. If they act as a substitute need, however, they become issues. Until we deal with the underlying blockage and return to our natural rhythms, we repeat the substitute needs for this little release and get stuck in a pattern. Sound familiar? You got it—we're back to identifying the Necessity.

Return to Feeling and Balance

Substitute needs aren't adequate for returning our body to balance. Not only do they provide only the barest release of blocked energy, they engage our mind in compounding the problem by adding on judgment, criticism, negative self-talk (*I really* shouldn't *eat another bowl of ice cream!*), or cognitive dissonance that tries to justifies it (this *ice cream is okay, it's organic*). As you can imagine, this mental activity itself takes energy, which means that our body energy becomes even more tangled. If you are thinking back to the piling up of Busy Dreams that we looked at in Chapter Three, you're right on target. Fortunately, we hold the tools to transform the situation.

Take a look again at Figure 3 a couple pages back. The image of the disbalanced state is what happens when no choice is made. Below that image, however, shows what happens when we choose to respond. This is the image of a balanced state, and it shows what happens when we channel our body energy to the place of **Feeling**. The decision to either end up in an emotion like fear or alternatively, a feeling like compassion happens in that little window I mentioned earlier, when we still have a choice whether we will react or respond.

Let's go back to the garden hose and the realization that we are the ones holding the hose. Holding the hose means we are the ones in charge of directing the flow of energy. It is through conscious intervention that we shift the movements of energy in our body from emotion to the feeling of our choice. But how do we consciously intervene, particularly when such movements are so quick? The answer lies in our body.

Mapping the Body

To work the Life Plan, we have to map our own bodies. We do this by identifying the specific experiences—the physical sensations, sense impressions, images, and other visceral aspects—of our primary instincts, emotions, and feelings. These detailed descriptions help us to clearly identify and demarcate each different experience. This, in turn, helps us to recognize when we've moved from one to another.

Let's say we pay attention to our breathing, and the sensations it produces, and find that rhythmic breathing is slow, belly-deep, and expansive, even with the color of crystal blue. That is a very specific experience, and the body knows it as such. Now that you've described it to yourself, your conscious mind—the one holding the garden hose—marks it as a specific experience also.

Now let's say you have a moment of anger. Pay attention to what is happening in your body. You may find that anger is an arrow-sharp tightening in the core, heaving breath, fast-moving, and red. This is a dramatically different experience than rhythmic breathing. Your body knows it, and now you do too.

Making the distinctions between rhythmic breathing and anger connects your thinking, willful self to your body experience, bringing to conscious awareness what is happening to you internally. That clarity means that you can catch the movement of energy the second it starts because the change is so apparent. This puts us squarely in the little window, ready to direct the energy from one place to another.

Each of the different experiences that we identify becomes a dot on our own neural-physiological map. Because they are physical, and we name them, they become an actual destination in our bodymind. That means that, just like a map, we can decide which destination we want to move to; we've been there before, we recognize it, and so we can go there again.

The more destinations we become consciously aware of on our map, the more choice we have. If my only strong recognitions are around anger, it is impossible to move somewhere else. With no other experienced, described, and named channel in which to send the energy, it's only going to go down the habitual path of anger. If, however, I have clearly identified what is happening in my body when I feel peaceful, calm, or some other feeling, and I have marked that as a destination, then I have a choice in what I do.

Each different emotion and feeling uses different neural circuitry and engages different cerebral regions.[8] The more we shift our energy to new destinations of feeling, the more we build and strengthen the neurosynaptic connections and body-memories involved with that choice.[9] This means that each subsequent time we make the shift it is *easier to do so*. We effectively trade in the pattern of reacting to challenge for the positive one of responding. Over time, we build a new way of being altogether.

Each of our body-states is known not only by our physical sensations, but also by image. We've seen already how images are formed to help us visualize the energies of our body. These images drive our behavior, and as neuroscientist Antonio Damasio has demonstrated, these images are not only specific to experience, they must be changed in order to consciously intervene in emotional regulation.[10] This we've also seen in numerous examples, from stopping an out-of-control car of overwhelm to jumping over a cardboard box in the way of a goal. Image is our key to all inner-knowing and change, and that's the next step of mapping our bodies: returning to the image.

Drawing Your Life Plan

Now we're at the point where you can begin to make your own personal Life Plan, using your own sensations, experiences, and images. We start with an imagery exercise. To do it, make sure you are in a place where you won't be disturbed. The exercise will take no longer than a minute, and make sure not to go longer than that. We are working with the spontaneous imagination and body energy, and both move quickly.

Sit comfortably, arms and legs uncrossed, and think of a recent time when you felt angry about something. Close your eyes, and feel and describe all the bodily sensations of this experience of anger. Is the body hot or cold, tense, constricted, rigid? Where, specifically, are these sensations? What other sensations do you have? Are there any colors or scents? What is the pace and tempo of the energy? What image do you have of this experience? Describe it.

Then, see that you have a strong garden broom and sweep all of these sensations out of your body and off to the left, and be sure to sweep the image off to the left also. Do it quick. Then, breathe out, and imagine turning 180 degrees and see the exact opposite image. Describe it and notice and describe also the sensations in your body as you see this exact opposite image. What is the rhythm now, the tempo, the character, and the direction of movement? What are the colors? The temperatures, the scents? Then, give a name to this experience. When you're done, breathe out, and open your eyes.

EXAMPLE OF BEGINNING TO FILL OUT INDIVIDUAL LIFE PLAN WITH IMAGES AND EXPERIENCES FROM IMAGERY EXERCISES

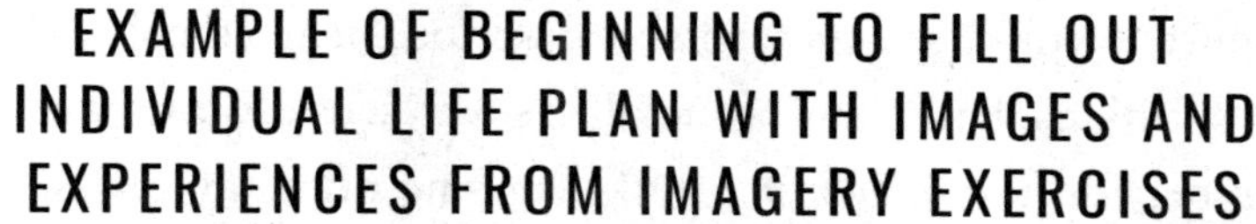

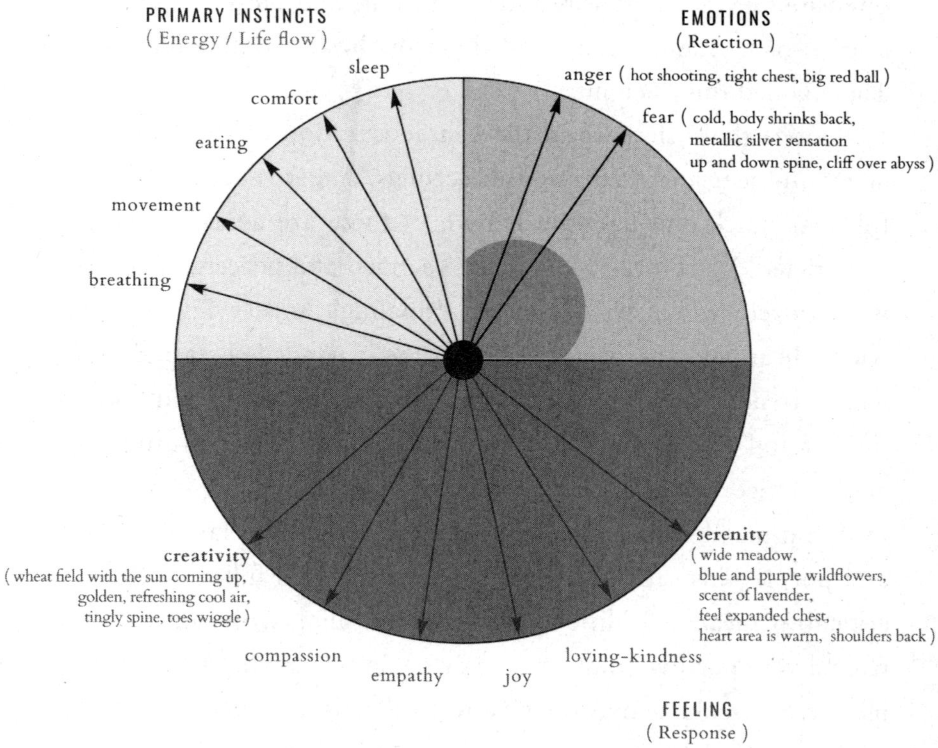

Figure 4

Once you've mapped these two experiences—anger, and its opposite (feeling)—put these on your Life Plan drawing. Figure 4 gives you an example of a Life Plan for someone at this beginning stage of filling it out. For them, anger was a hot, shooting sensation, and a tight chest, with the image of a big, red ball. The opposite of this is a golden wheat field with the sun coming up, and the bodily sensations of cool air, tingly spine, and wiggling toes, which they named "Creativity."

The next step is to do the exact same exercise, this time with fear. When you've done it, add this also to your Life Plan drawing. In Figure 4 you'll see that person described fear as cold, with the body shrinking back, and a metallic silver sensation up and down the spine, and the image of a cliff dropping off to an abyss. For its opposite they describe a meadow with blue and purple wildflowers, a scent of lavender, an expanded warm chest, and shoulders back. They named this "Serenity."

Notice the difference in the characterization of the energies of anger and fear and their opposite feelings. Anger is acute and forceful, fear quick and backward; both of these are concentrated and constricted. By contrast, feeling is expanded and peaceful, and yet it is energized, which we see in the "tingling" and "wiggling." The wide wheat field and meadow mirror the expanded chest and movement of energy; the moderated temperatures of warm and cool vs. the hot and cold of anger and fear inform us also of a return to balance. Notice, too, the enlarged spectrum of experience—the wheat field and meadow contain numerous colors: golden, lavender, blue, and purple—instead of just red or metallic. This fuller spectrum is critical; it means the difference between dealing with our problems from a very narrow point of view or having the ability to see the big picture and make connections between details and events.

Emotion concentrates our neural activity away from our higher cognitive faculties, hamstringing our ability to solve problems.[11] When we shift our energy, we shift our ability to work through the challenge that first knocked us out of balance. This means that *just* shifting our energy has enormous repercussions. Without needing to dig and sort through specifics of a challenge before we can deal with them, moving our energy to a place of feeling automatically puts us in position of being able to resolve it, no matter what the specifics are.

The lens through which we approach a challenge—emotion or feeling—determines outcome. Reactive decisions will, inherently, be as narrow and constricted as our inner energy, influencing our ability to view the situation fully. Channeling our energy to feeling allows us to bring in multiple considerations, like the multiple colors of the purple, blue, golden in the example, and creatively resolve challenge. From the point of view of finding the Necessity, whether it is a life challenge or energy that has been disturbed in the Life Plan, in both cases consciously managing our energy is the Necessity. After that, resolves will become evident.

Shifting energy from emotion to feeling is as easy as the exercise at the start of this chapter; easier, now that you've done it. Because you have the image of the feeling you want to have, when you sense the onset of an emotion, simply exhale and see in your mind's eye the image of your feeling. Pay attention to the shifts it brings in your body, then exhale again and continue going about your day. Once a feeling image has been identified, you can make this shift with your eyes open. Even while sitting in a tense meeting or opening an explosive email on your phone in public, you can still soften your gaze, exhale, see the image of feeling, and make the shift. No one has to know but you.

Eating Ice Cream and Other Substitute Needs

Now that you've started your body-mapping with anger, fear, and their opposite feelings, let's tackle the substitute needs part of the Life Plan. We do that with a three-column exercise.

3 COLUMN EXERCISE

EMOTION *can be primary or secondary*	REACTION *« What I do » Substitute need*	WHAT I LIKE

Chart

Get a notebook that you can carry around with you, and mark off three columns. You can see an example of this in this chart. The left column is the emotion, which can be primary or secondary, and the middle column is the "what I do," or the reactionary substitute need. These two always go together. For example, I would get increasingly tense writing my dissertation, breathing less and less and not moving from in front of my computer, until I was—what I named—just plain anxious. Then—up! —I would walk to the freezer and make a bowl of ice cream to calm back down. So for me, I would write *anxious* in the far left column and *eat ice cream* in the center column. For other people, it may be *angry at kids*, then *go online and scroll mindlessly for thirty minutes*.

The reason for having the three columns side by side and in a notebook you carry around with you is to start to identify the patterns of these emotions and reactions. Remember it wasn't the first bowl of ice cream I ate that was a problem—it was that I did it *every day*. By tracking each emotion and reaction as it happens, we build a case, like a detective. Writing them down in the moment means that we catch each occurrence—it may be that several times in the day you go online to scroll, or eat a chocolate bar at your desk, or bite your nails. Or, one minute it may be anxiety and shopping, and later in the day anger and making a snarky online post. If we trust it to memory, we'll invariably miss something and lose important data.

Now the column for "what I like." This column sits next to the others but will not be filled in at the same time as the others. It's pretty hard to like something while in the throes of an emotion. We'll get to why we put it here in a minute. For now, the things that go into that column are things you like, written down also in the moment that they happen. Let's say you wake up to let the dog out and catch a brilliant sunrise that captivates you. This would go in the column—*brilliant sunrise*—as well as what you feel when experiencing it. Maybe you say you feel refreshed, awake, joy, the rising up of energy along your spine. Maybe later in the day you step into a store to buy a gift and a citrus-scented soap grabs your attention, giving you the bodily sensation of "sparkling" and a giggle—that goes in the third column, too. What's important is to note each specific moment, as it happens, rather than thinking through general things you already know you like.

Set aside a full week to do your observation with the three columns. When you are done, take a look back at the first two columns and see if one thing appears more frequently than the others. For example, does anger show up over and over again, or is it fear, or anxiety? Does one particular pattern of an emotion paired with a substitute need feature more prominently? Then take a look at the overall view and see how frequently or infrequently you have placed items in the "what I like" column. If there aren't very many, and the first two columns far outweigh what you've placed in the third, that can be a clue that it's time to work the Life Plan. Fortunately, the tool is built into the exercise.

Knowing your reactionary substitute needs, just like knowing the bodily sensations of emotion and its opposite, sets the stage for changing them. The key is the third column which, as you've guessed, is the column of *feeling*. In a more tangible sense, the third column activities can help you break patterns around emotions and reactions. When you catch yourself starting an activity that you have put in the second column—scrolling, shopping, or so on—pause a moment and see if it is connected to an emotion. Identify it, then do something from the "what I like" column instead. Notice how that consciously redirects the energy.

I broke the pattern of eating the ice cream every day by walking my dog around the block. I really loved taking my dog for a walk, and so each time I began to feel the rising tension of the dissertation I would step away from the computer, put her on a leash, and off we would go for a quick round. My neighbors probably wondered why we were suddenly looping the neighborhood several times a day, but she loved it and I put myself back in balance.

Knowing that energy is just energy takes the pressure off recognizing which emotions we have habitually directed it to. It also makes it easier to change that habit and put the energy to a more beneficial use. When we see the force of anger as energy, for example, we can recognize that very same force as passionate joy. Without critical self-judgment, we can simply name the channel and decide to find a different one.

One last note: shifting an emotion is not the same thing as stuffing it. Stuffing energy consigns it to a secondary emotion. A true shift occurs by being present to, and working with, the energy to move it somewhere else. Experience shifts the body entirely; only then do we return to balance.[12]

Mapping our bodies, and identifying new destinations, isn't always immediately apparent. Our dreams, however, help us, giving us yet another window into our inner experience. In the next section we'll look at how our dreams correspond to the Life Plan.

Dreams and the Life Plan

At the top of this chapter is a dream with patterns of *red* and *rocky*. Red dirt, red boulders, and a deep red canyon that narrows. This dream sits neatly on the Life Plan as a primary emotion. Rocky red and narrowed canyon, if we sense into it, feels a lot like hot, concentrated anger. The intensity of energy is seen in the truck that keeps shoving forward, over the *big* rocks.

The movements and blockages of our energy—the different phases of the Life Plan—and the inner images they create appear as the seven different kinds of dreams we looked at in Chapter Three. Figure 5 shows the seven kinds of dreams mapped onto the Life Plan. Overlaying the two gives you both a daytime (Life Plan) and nighttime (dreaming) orientation device. In addition, the images of the dreams, and their visceral nature, help you to add details and new destinations as you draw your own Life Plan.

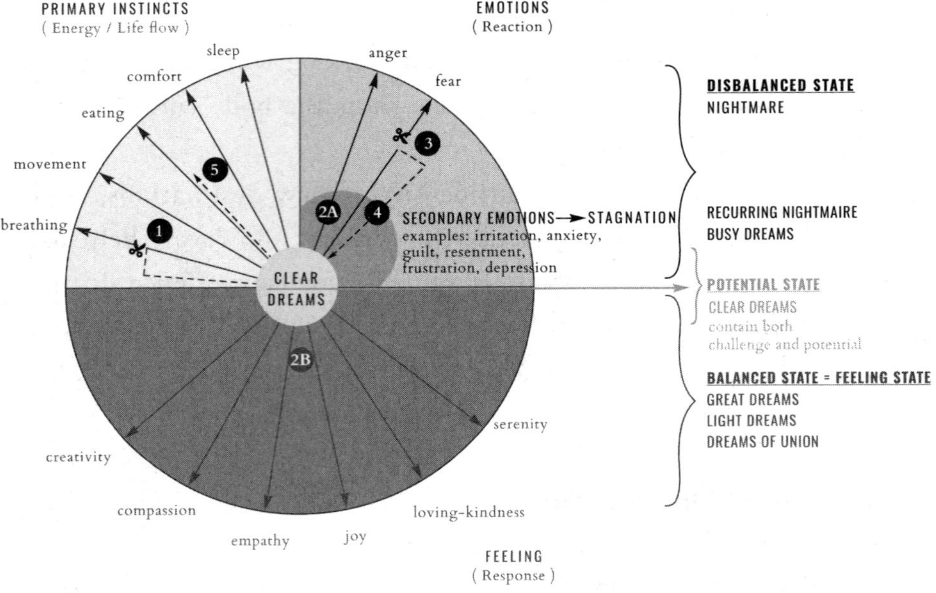

Figure 5

Nightmares, like the dream of the big red rocks, belong next to the primary emotions on the Life Plan. We would put the big red rocks next to anger. Earlier in the book we encountered a dreamer razing a stadium of people with a flamethrower—we'd put that dream there too.

The dark house, with the dreamer outside afraid to go in, belonged to fear the *first* time it was dreamed. It so happens that this dream became a recurring NIGHTMARE, which would place it in the secondary emotions section of the Life Plan.

The Busy Dream we looked at in a previous chapter was a waking time scenario of the executive who was piling on, thinking he needed to find a new job (but at the same time thinking he would never be hired). His cocktail of frustration, resentment, and anxiety had brought him to a standstill. That standstill mirrors the stagnant secondary emotions of the Life Plan, which is the section where Busy Dreams also belong.

One note about Busy Dreams: these dreams can also occur if our body is undergoing a physical event such as a fever or the hormonal irregularities of menopause, or if we are taking medications. Any of these are changes introduced to the body system, and the body has a response to that. While these changes may be part of the healing process, the dreaming will still reflect where we are in that process; the body is busy with a lot of input, and the dreams may be busy also.

What about the dream of the red pepper, or the dancer who steps out, or even the waking dream exercise of the golden almond with the cardboard box in the way? Each of these are Clear Dreams and they sit at the very center of potential. They are *the window* where we can go either way. Each of these dreams had a tangled emotion: the red pepper included sadness and jealousy, the dancer had the fear of the terrifying couch-turned-man, and the cardboard box was mental anxiety. And yet, these dreams each also contained elements of feeling: the red pepper with the warmth, dancing, hugging; the dancer with the expansive beach horizon; the golden almond, which the dreamer said felt like freedom, on the other side of the box. In each, the dreamer's window for choosing either emotion or feeling was open. Their internal balance had been disrupted, but the outcome had not yet been decided. That decision would lie in what the dreamer decided to do with the dream upon waking; either they move toward or ignore the red pepper; step into the dance or stay frozen; take the almond or let the box stop them.

Shifting our energy to response returns us to feeling and an expanded spectrum of experience. This state generates Great Dreams,

Light Dreams, and Dreams of Union, which sit on the feeling section on the Life Plan. Frequently, these dreams have impressive images that inspire us. We can use these images like the third column to help us break patterns in waking time.

One client had the surprise of seeing a specific talisman in a waking dream exercise which he then searched for, and found, in waking life. When he knew at one point that he was going to have a difficult conversation with his boss, he put the talisman in his pocket, touching it with his hand as they talked, to remind him of where he wanted to send his energy: a destination he called "Courage." Instead of a forecasted dead end, the conversation led to a new role for himself with more pay.

One more tool that will help you to create a new destination for your energy is to title your dreams. Do it after you have worked with the Necessity of the dream to bring it from unresolved to resolved. Titles are like naming the experience of feeling, and they mark the fact that something has been overcome: the challenge and the imbalance was present, the Necessity was addressed, and it was overcome to arrive at a new, balanced place. The title becomes like the chapter of the adventure book of your life. "Flying High," "Growing Tall," and "Finding the Golden Necklace" are examples from clients.

The Life Plan, used in concert with our dreams, gives us a full toolbox for navigating our life. When used, we become conscious creators of our life. Each shift we make not only brings us back to balance, it restores our ability to have a Great Dream. The next section of the book takes a look at what is possible when we become Great Dreamers.

CHAPTER NINE

Dreaming While Awake: Your Intuiting Self

"I am in a plant store and, as I am paying the cashier, I feel an 'inner push,' really like someone pushes me from the inside, and I hear or 'know' the sentence: "Ask them about the vet." Even though it's totally incongruous—it's a plant store—I say, "I've been looking for a veterinarian who does natural healing, holistic in some way—do you know anyone?" The cashier looks at me strangely. "Actually, I do. That's weird that's come up again this week. I know of two." She writes down two names on a piece of paper and slides it over. I look, and one name stands out a little brighter, and my body feels relaxed to see it. I make an appointment with this 'brighter' vet, and finally, after four months of trying different vets, to no avail, this one knows how to heal my dogs."

—Dreamer

What does it mean when we know something before it happens?

Chapter Three looked at the seven kinds of dreams, but there is another kind of experience we have that expresses our inner knowing in a different way. It appears in our night dreams as a premonition, and in waking time as intuition. Both are the same. We feel them as unique, however, and they carry their own special call to action. In general, when we have the experience of intuiting or predicting something, it is an exciting sign that we are waking up to our dreaming. The more you work with your dreaming, the more you will begin to have intuitive experiences. In this chapter, we'll look under the hood at where these experiences come from, how to develop them, how to distinguish them from other experiences in our lives, and what to do with them.

Knowing More than You Think

As we saw in Chapter Two, dreaming is a part of our experiencing and our response to experience. It contains awareness and cognitive processing beyond what we focus on with our direct, conscious attention. The body-mind that produces dreams gathers data from things like our body's location in space and where other things are located relative to that. It also gathers data from our senses, like what we smell and hear while typing away at work. When we are focused on work, we may think we are blocking those senses out, but light a fire in the trashcan of someone's office down the hall and the scent of smoke and the strange crackling sounds will pull us away from the keyboard. No matter how much we might think our attention is solely centered on a task at hand, our bodies are busily gathering information beyond it. Perception just outside our conscious attention is what William James called the "fringe".[1] It's a distinct form of noticing, interacting with, and understanding our environment.[2]

I grew up with a story from my father that is a perfect example. When he was a young boy in Texas, one day he was with his father at the family farm and asked to borrow his father's knife so he could whittle a piece of wood. His father said yes, but that he had to give it back at dinner. No problem. Dinner came, however, and my dad didn't have the knife—he had completely forgotten about it. He ran out to the barn and searched in a panic until late in the evening and couldn't find it anywhere. Finally, his mother came out and told him that he had looked enough and that it was time to go to bed. As she tucked him in, she told him that if he asked his dreams, they would show him.

My father went to sleep, and in his dream he sees himself walking the fence line, counting fence posts. One. . . Two. . . Three. . . He goes on until he gets to a certain number, and then he stretches his arm his above his head—in the way that dreams allow us to stretch far higher than we normally could—and he feels the knife on top of that post. He wakes up and runs out in the dark to the fence line and starts counting off posts: One. . . Two. . . Three. . . All the way to the number in his dream. Then he climbs up, and there, on top of the fence post, exactly as his dream had shown him, was the knife!

While my father had at some point in his day climbed on top of the fence and set the knife down in plain view, later back on the ground the knife was well out of his sight. His curious little-boy, thinking self immediately forgot about it as he went from whittling wood to playing with the horses, to every next thing that caught his interest throughout the day. Though his logical-thinking mind completely forgot about it, his *body* knew quite well where, when, and how everything had transpired. The logical mind was further clouded by the panicked emotion of disappointing his father and getting punished, but when he relaxed into dreaming, he was able to reaccess that inner space of embodied knowing.

Dreams, intuition, and premonitory dreams are all three different facets of the same whole: our body's ability to pay attention to, attend to, and process the vast amount of information it encounters.

Most everyone I've met has had at least one intuitive or premonitory experience in their life. It's sometimes difficult to express the experiences of them though. They include sensations and happenings for which we don't have adequate vocabulary. This uncanny nature is also, well, *weird*; my clients tell me about their premonitions in a hushed, confessional manner.

"Strange" is only strange, though, because it is not everyday, logically verified, or causal; we can't say that "X" happened because of "Y." Intuitive knowledge seems to come from out of nowhere. Because of this, we hesitate to talk about these experiences with others. We also wonder if we can trust them.

The question of whether we can trust our intuition comes from having once been separated from it, usually as children. Children are naturally intuitive and very connected to the dream world. Unfortunately, many parents, teachers, and other adults dismiss the inner experiences that children have because they seem to not make sense. This is because children speak in image. When they report, for example, that at lunch a terrifying black swan flew into the playground, scattering the kids, this is not made up—it really happened. The black swan may be the substitute teacher, the principal, or some other seemingly frightening aspect of their day.

Children continue to be connected to their intuition and speak this dreaming language until education begins in earnest and they shift to developing the logical, rational mind. Dreaming and intuition never go away, though. They're always with us. And, just like developing a dreaming practice, we can learn to develop our intuition. Because they are the same thing, this development goes hand in hand. It begins as the dreaming practice does: by deciding to be open to having these experiences without expectation, judgment, or criticism, and to view them with curiosity.

I was lucky to have been raised by a father and grandmother who were Great Dreamers. We have many family stories about intuition and premonitory dreams like the one I recounted above. We talked about them in our family, and so they were normal. I told my family my dreams and they were listened to. My father also gave me countless imagery and intuition-building exercises that developed my connection to my body and inner-knowing. Because it was supported from early on, I've been able to build an enormous database of experiences that document for myself how dreaming and intuition work as an internal phenomenon and as an external event.

Interestingly, at my institute we have a children's program and one of the exercises we give is to have the children ask their parents to tell them a dreaming story. We've never had a child return without one. Often, they are intuition-based or premonitory dreams—knowing which college acceptance will come in, or the person that will be their partner. Many include knowing they are about to be pregnant with the very child asking them to tell them the story, including knowing if they will be a boy or girl. We get a lot of emotional feedback on this homework from the parents, and many wonder why they never shared these dreams with their kids.

In this exercise, the parents could name these dreams as premonitory because something had already happened to verify it: the dream that generated the inner knowing that a college acceptance would come in was determined to be premonitory when the letter came in the mail; the premonition of getting pregnant was proved by getting pregnant. But what about before the proof arrives—how do we know if we are getting an intuitive message or having a premonitory dream?

A "Different" Kind of Dream

Even though intuition and premonitory dreams are part of the overall dreaming fabric, they are also distinct in specific ways. They are distinguished by a unique quality—how they *feel*—which is innately understood as "different" by the dreamer. How, specifically, it is different depends on who is dreaming—each person will feel and experience it differently in their own bodies. Describing that difference, though, often defies our known vocabulary.

At the top of the chapter is a waking-time intuition story from my own experience. In that experience I felt "pushed from the inside," "knowing a sentence," and seeing a name that is "brighter than another," though both were written in the same ink on the same piece of paper. These are not everyday, regular experiences, and I struggled with how to express them. What does it mean to feel pushed from the inside? To see a name that is "brighter"? The other challenge in describing this experience is that it happened very quickly, almost "all at once," a flash of total, holistic knowing that is a hallmark of intuitive experiences.

Even though everyday vocabulary is inadequate, and I still haven't quite captured the otherworldly quality of this experience, I can definitively say this was not a fantasy or mentally made-up thought because each of the qualities I mention are deeply embodied. I was, quite unexpectedly, "pushed." The knowing I describe is deep in my core, like a settling. The brightness of the name was an actual visual event for me, not a trick of the eye. And the sped-up time is only known as fast because my body is familiar with a certain way that time usually moves.

A waking intuitive experience is easy to differentiate from regular waking time because of its unique, felt qualities and its strangeness. Night dreams already have strange elements, though. So, how do we tell the difference between "regular" dreams and premonitory ones?

Like waking intuitive experiences, premonitory night dreams will also feel different. Your body won't experience them in the ways that you think of as more "regular" dreams. Getting clear on that comes from experience, though.

I think of it like this: the people who live above the Arctic Circle make numerous distinctions between different kinds of snow—there is slippery snow, dry snow, dry snow on top of ice, and so on. Each of these appearances of snow has its own name. To most of us south of the Arctic Circle, it's "just snow." Those above the Arctic Circle know the difference, though, because of their experience touching, tasting, hearing, smelling, seeing, and moving through snow so regularly. Dreaming is the same. The more we dream, the more varied our dream experiences will be, and the easier it will be to make distinctions between them.

I'll give you some tips at the end of the chapter for developing your repository of experience so that you can fine-tune your ability to differentiate intuitive experiences and premonitory dreams from regular waking or dreaming experiences.

Here's a premonitory dream of mine:

I am in the bottom of a swimming pool, looking up at the surface. Plunging into the pool is a newborn baby boy. I catch him in my arms, and we swim together to the surface where my friend Joan is. I hand her the baby.

I wake from this dream and know that my friend Joan is pregnant. I also know that the child is a boy. The dream had an "extra-sensory" quality to it; all the nerve-endings of my body were turned on like little satellite dishes getting signals at the same time. It had a particular visceral experience of full-body expansion. There was a heightened vividness—the colors were more intense, the water more crystal blue, the sun brighter than any waking time experience, and more vivid than the everyday colors found in a Clear Dream. Time, too, had a different quality, that I could almost touch—a bit like stepping into an iridescent bubble that was a moment lifted out of time. I knew it was a dream, yet it felt like I was living a future event that was really happening.

All of these descriptions seem to point toward a premonitory dream. Many of these qualities however, like the extreme vividness, are also similar to those of a Great Dream. This could have been a Great Dream of my own, where Joan is an aspect of me, and the birthing is something that's happening in my waking life, like a new aspect of myself emerging. How to tell the difference?

While the vividness of the premonitory dream could have been a Great Dream, it still had a quality that seemed "just different" —it was vivid, yet not "Great Dream vivid." The time event aspect of the dream was also unique. These differences helped me to differentiate it. I was only able to make that distinction, though, because I have a lot of experience writing down my dreams and daytime intuitive experiences. The more you work with your dreams, the more these distinctions will become clear to you, too.

Knowing Beyond Ourselves: Responding to Intuition and Premonitory Dreams

In the story about my father and the lost knife, the dream reflected back information that he had, earlier in the day, lived. In the dream with my friend Joan, however, I had not previously lived any part of that dream. Neither did we ever talk about her and her husband trying to get pregnant. At that particular moment in her life, Joan was very focused on her career and a recent promotion—pregnancy was far off my radar when thinking about her. And yet, I got some kind of information about her, anyway. How?

While each of us are unique individuals, living a unique life, we also all share the human experience and are thus all connected on some level. In fact, all of life is interconnected.[3] Everything that we see as separate—atoms and electrons, for example—is part of a larger whole. Go up or down in levels, and all parts are embedded in larger, organized systems, something called Nested Hierarchies.[4]

Like a giant web, information travels along these connections, and is able to be received, even if to our eyes this information, and the events generating it, seem separated by time and space. Quantum physicists call this the quantum field, but I tend to call it the dream field.

Because this deep well of information isn't limited by material bounds, we can tune in to the vibration of things that are happening to other beings on the planet. We can also sense things that are coming into form and manifestation before they quite get there; ideas, beginning to vibrate at more intense frequencies, spin off information even as they progress toward finding a tangible expression, like watching clouds build and knowing a change of weather is approaching. When we dip into this larger space of awareness we call it intuition or a premonitory dream.

Because intuitions and premonitory dreams often seem to disclose information about the future, they feel like they are asking us to do something about that information, not just receive it. The big question is how. In the dream example above, I know my friend Joan is pregnant, but do I tell her? Do I let her know it will be a boy?

All dreams ask us to respond to them, and that responsiveness is a key theme of this book. In the intuition experience at the top of the chapter, I responded to the inner push by asking the cashier at the plant store if they could recommend a holistic vet, even though I knew that was not their area of expertise. When in front of the two names, I responded to the second intuitive flash of seeing one as brighter. I called the one whose name appeared brighter and made an appointment. I wasn't "sold" on the brighter vet until I could meet her. I approached the appointment with all ears open to hear what might arrive. Because the meeting was instigated by my intuition, for all I knew the vet might have a piece of information I needed to hear that had nothing to do with my dogs.

Intuition is not linear, and we need to stay open and alert to what might come our way, following the trail like breadcrumbs through the forest. In this case the vet was the first professional to finally know what was wrong with my dogs and heal them. That's pretty linear. But she also, surprisingly, became an important friend, present and supportive in countless ways in my life, which I could never add up in a linear fashion. Were the sick dogs pretext to make the connection for the friendship? Did the friendship "just happen" coincidentally? Following our intuition leads down unexpected trails that can open many doors if we stay open and don't rush to close or define it at the first linear correspondence.

Responding to an intuition about oneself is rather straightforward. Some intuitive experiences and premonitory dreams, though, involve people other than ourselves. It's one thing to have a dream or intuition and understand for the self that it's time to take a new job or call a vet, but quite another to think of a message for someone else. That gets into tricky territory, so we have to be careful how we deal with this kind of information, starting with making sure it really *is* about someone else.

I posed the question of whether the dream about Joan was premonitory about her pregnancy, or if it was a Great Dream giving me a message about something birthing in myself. In other words, was this about Joan, or an aspect of me that "Joan" in the dream was showing up as? Asking such a question is an initial filter we can use to sort between premonitory and other dreams.

It is easy to unknowingly add our own interpretations to premonitions, particularly if we feel a strong emotion around what it is we've intuited, for example, if we feel ecstatic for our friend that she is pregnant. Our emotions, mental constructs, biases, investment in outcome, and other ideas, are inner noise that obstruct our listening. We have to filter out the noise to get a clear message. Quite simply, we have to know what is ours and what isn't.

We also have to remember that the information that comes to us in all its many forms—waking time perceptions, regular dreams, intuitions, or premonitory dreams—is like any other sense information in our environment. Each one of us is going to receive it differently, like one person picking up the hint of lemon in a chicken soup and the other being oblivious to it, because they are focused, instead, on the cilantro.

So, what did I do with the dream about Joan being pregnant? Nothing! I didn't *need* to do anything, as there was no call to action in this dream. My possible knowledge was simply something received.

Joan was now in my mind, though, so I did respond by simply calling her and asking how she was doing. That's it—only that one simple question. If I had told her the dream, I would have crossed a boundary into her own unfolding experience. The call was a neutral invitation. It turns out she was glad I called because she was excited to tell me that she had just found out the day before that she was pregnant. She also told me that she and her husband had decided they wanted to be surprised about the gender until the birth itself. Thankfully I hadn't said anything about the dream, especially any details, because I would have blown the fun surprise if I had mentioned the baby boy. When she gave birth to that boy eight months later, I just made note of it as a confirmation—only to myself, though, to further my own relationship with my intuition and dreaming. Maintaining boundaries is key to responding to an intuition or premonitory dream. Calling someone to ask how they are is usually all we have to do—if we feel we have to do anything at all.

Dreaming is ultimately about freedom—freeing ourselves from patterns or old belief systems that hold us in place, and freeing ourselves from our own inhibiting tendencies that keep us from fully expressing ourselves. This also means ensuring freedom for everyone else and not making assumptions that might curtail their free expression.

We have to be careful not to ring a bell that can't be un-rung. Even though we may have picked up on information, it doesn't mean that the other person has yet, or is ready to.

There's another element, too, around interrupting possibility. The moment we speak aloud information from a premonition, we acknowledge something that is potential but not yet actualized. Speaking aloud is itself something tangible—it takes something inchoate and brings it closer to form. If something is in a potential state, things can still go in other directions. Once we hear something, however, our mind attaches an image to it and a response—this is the bell that can't be un-rung. Speaking aloud an intuition makes it an actual thing the other person now has to deal with: either they deny it, accept it, or rebel against it. What people tell us sticks in our mind, and from mental ideas we create actions. There's an old saying that "dreams follow the mouth";[5] what we interpret and say has weight.

It is common for new dreamers to dream of someone they know well and confuse it with a premonitory dream. This is especially the case if it is accompanied by aspects that correspond to waking life, and even more so if the dream has heightened emotions. The emotional and visceral aspects of these dreams appear to be pushing us to action in some way because they "feel so real!"

Dreaming is exciting. The vivid, visceral experiences of night dreams—as well as daytime synchronicities and intuitions—will increase the more you work with your dreams. These are signs that we are becoming more embodied and present to our self and the world around us. Not all our more vivid night dreams are necessarily premonitory. Most night dreams—including those who feature someone we know in waking life—will be dreams about our own self. They may carry a new perspective around a waking life situation and person, but that isn't the same thing as foretelling a future event.

The example with Joan is a good-news kind of premonition. Sometimes, though, we might intuit that someone is not doing well, or, in very rare cases, may even be in danger. In these cases, the same "call and ask how they are" response holds true, though our response may need to be extra swift. Often just the call is what a person going through a difficult time needs most.

Knowing what we are dreaming, and whether it is about us or someone else, all comes back to the physical body. The more you dream, the more you will know how to tell the difference between different dream experiences. We can also develop our intuition with some fun practices, which is where we go next.

Becoming a Scientist of Your Intuiting Self—Practices to Grow Your Intuition

Intuition, like dreaming, is subtle. Unlike a loud, attention-grabbing billboard, signals from our inner intuition require a finer-tuned ear to catch. It uses a different, embodied communication that may have any combination of sounds, words, emotions, feelings, and more. We get present to these communications by becoming present to our bodies.

Each person has their own specific relationship to their intuition. A friend of mine feels a particular shock of "cold electric" down her spinal column, another speaks about the quality of time, that it "slows down" like suddenly being "in a bubble" (a bit like I described in my dream above). I mentioned feeling "pushed from the inside," "knowing a sentence," and seeing a name that was brighter than another. I also often experience the color silver when I have an intuition, and like my friend, time can move exceptionally slow or super-fast. It may be marked by sound or sudden silence. Identifying how your own body receives intuition is the first step in creating and strengthening your relationship to it. It begins by describing sensation.

Noticing and describing the physical sensations of your intuitive moments takes being a bit of a scientist. It involves taking down all the details, much of which will come from contrasting and comparing intuitive moments with other experiences. So, we have to go out exploring to do a bit of research.

First, start to notice what you physically experience around making regular, daily decisions. These probably feel flatter, not very viscerally engaging, and not as unique as intuition, which is going to be distinctive in some way to grab your attention—like a shiver down the spine. By getting clear on what happens in regular decision-making, we establish a sort of "control group" for our work as self-scientists.

The next step is to get a specific intuition journal, different from your dream one. Record any moment that you feel that you have a sense of intuition about something, including the time and date, and all the sensations and other details of how it moves in your body. This may be a little pull to go out to dinner with a friend, a sense to give someone a call, or a yen to turn right instead of left and take a circular route home instead of the usual one. Then, write in your journal how you choose to respond to this intuition, even if that response is to *not* follow its message.

Recording how we choose to respond to intuitive messages—or if our choice is to *not* respond—is how we get confirmation. These confirmations verify the intuiting process, taking it out of the murky realm of trust and into a lived, observed phenomenon.

We can't confirm our intuition, however, unless it is written down as close to when we experience it as possible. Time makes us hazy with details; either we forget things, or we unknowingly reconstruct events according to emotions, doubts, desires and other intrusive obstructions. Just like a scientist, we have to objectively record *as we observe.*

The last step is to record how the intuition eventually unfolds. I put mine on the same page where I wrote the initial experience, using a pen with a different color of ink; this makes it easier to flip back through and reference. Be sure to put the time and date, and any other details of the unfolding, which will be an important part of your verification process.

Once I was walking my dog before sunrise. As we were walking, the image of my friend Mary wearing a pink robe suddenly appeared in front of me, along with a strong feeling—positive, without danger—to call her. It was well into morning before I got to it, by the time I returned home, fed the dog, and had my own breakfast. She picked up the call saying she had woken up with me strongly in her mind and had planned to call me later that day. I asked what she was wearing—she said a gray dress. That was unexpected, because my image had been so clear, so I asked what time she had thought of me so strongly and she said it was "really right when I woke up. I was in my pink robe, brushing my teeth, and pop: there you were!" Aha, there was a pink robe after all! This detail was *the* confirmation.

I responded to the image of my friend Mary and the feeling to call her by doing just that. Not responding, however, is often a sore teaching for learning to do so. We receive the teaching, however, only if we are careful to note it.

I was once overseeing the restoration of a one-story historic home. One day, as I was there to check in on the team, and as soon as I stepped onto the property, I immediately saw across my visual field, in black all-capital letters, "TELL THEM ABOUT THE LADDER." I felt all the physical sensations that distinguish intuition for me, including a different sense of time. I didn't, however, respond by heeding the message. Instead, I glanced around the property and checked to see that everything was in safe order. I let my thinking mind intrude, and thought about the fact that it was a simple one-story home. Mentally, I did not see any danger, so I let my logical mind talk myself out of it.

As I continued around the site, chatting with the team, however, my intuition kept repeating the phrase loudly in my ears—"TELL THEM ABOUT THE LADDER." Again, I didn't respond, and instead walked the full property, inspecting everything, signing off to the safety of it from my own visual observation, and still not saying what my intuition was urging me to say. I left the property with the statement continuing in my body-ear. By the time I had walked the few blocks home I had fourteen messages on my phone: one of our team had fallen off a ladder and an iron stake had pierced his bicep.

This is a dramatic example of an intuition and direct and immediate confirmation. Thankfully, our team member is perfectly okay. I wrote the whole experience in my notebook and my relationship with my intuition, as you might imagine, is forever changed and deepened.

When Newton had a sense that an unseen property existed—what we now know as gravity—he dropped apple after apple, which fell to the ground time after time, and affirmed this unseen presence. In the same way, we can confirm intuition's unseen presence through careful observation and verification of its effects. Writing down how and when intuition unfolds lets you to go back through your notebook—even months or years later—and keep track of how your intuitive dreaming is an active presence in your life. You may be surprised to find the paths it has helped you to chart for yourself.

When we fine-tune our relationship to our intuition and dreaming, we can be intentional about using it to make changes in our lives. In the next chapter we look at this, following a dream journey.

CHAPTER TEN

Great Dreaming: Manifesting a Dreaming Journey

"I dream a signpost on my left that says 'Warwickshire,' my friend Myri standing next to it; on my right, my dream teacher at a table with a tarot spread. She fans out the cards and throws them in the air. I see they've turned into playing cards and I notice two: an ace or eight of diamonds, and an ace or three of spades. I wake up and know my life has just completely changed."

—DREAMER

Chapter One began with a dream of a horse and carriage coming down the side of the River Seine toward the dreamer, then a red motorboat zipping away from her. The dreamer awoke knowing she could no longer wait to pursue her dream of writing and art, and immediately quit her job. Soon after, she found a new job as a journalist covering the arts: the two loves, combined. How did the message of this dream give the dreamer the conviction to make such a huge life change?

We've spent most of this book looking at how dreams show us where we are in our present tense, and the blocks we are currently facing. Sometimes, though, dreams surprise us with a life-changing message that seems to reach far beyond our everyday. This chapter looks at how to work with these Great Dreams, including asking for confirmations, both in dream and waking time, building on the intuitive work of the last chapter. If we let them, these Great Dreams take us on a journey. We'll start with a Great Dream journey of mine, which led to my moving from my home in the US to France, a country I knew little about, wasn't interested in, and in which I didn't speak the language. And yet, somehow, my dreams knew it was the next perfect adventure for me.

Catching the Moment

In 2011, I began to sense a change in the air. Eventually, a thought arose in me around moving. This was surprising—I had just finished renovating my home and was deeply involved with my community and a close circle of friends. And yet, like an October day that arrives unexpectedly clear and crisp, turning attention from summer to autumn, I woke one morning with a surprise inner shift that had me feeling it was time to move. Where? I had no desire to live in another place. And yet, time and change were already in motion somewhere deep inside of me.

Our body's relationship to time and change goes hand in hand with our intuition; feeling that it is the right time to go to graduate school, for example, or knowing when one has come to the end of a certain life chapter. Like nature that is tethered to the seasons, there are certain moments when our own development is ready to be furthered. *Being a dreamer is knowing how to catch a moment.*[1] By being present to inner movements around time and change, we are ready to take opportunities when they arrive, like learning to feel the undercurrents in the ocean, and getting in position on a surfboard, long before the appearance of a wave.

When we sense a change, we can actively engage it with our dreaming. This is another way that we become responsive, awake dreamers in our lives. One way to do this is what I call "walking the dream." Like taking a dog out on an interesting, meandering trail, walking a dream means taking the still-unformed sense impression about something into the crucible of waking life. For me it started, in fact, with a real dog.

Each weekend I regularly met a friend for a long hike with our dogs at a nature preserve near where she lived. The next time I drove to meet her, it occurred to me that living near downtown as I did might not be as appealing as living somewhere with access to hikes that I could take more regularly. Walking the dream of this new bit of information, I started to visit different suburbs outside the city center. I explored with dreamer's ears and eyes, acutely attuned to my sensing self in each location, and paying attention to any synchronicities or clues that might arrive. Months went by and nothing popped up; no place I went felt like a fit, and my night dreaming was silent on the subject.

I cast a wider net. I thought it might be nice to live closer to family back in Texas where I grew up, and I set up a dreaming trip to visit. There, everything checked off "on paper": it was a nice-sized city, with ample outdoor areas for hiking, and family and old friends lived there. I was heavily leaning in that direction. So, I decided to test it.

After lunch downtown one day, I put myself in my most aware, attentive state, actively connecting with my dreaming. I said out loud "this is exactly like what a regular day here would be for me. I would lunch with a friend, then get in the car, and drive back home." As I drove back to my brother's house just outside the city, I kept saying things out loud, like “this is the road I would take” or “this is the intersection I would cross” or “this is the building I would pass.” I was both feeling for my body’s response to these statements, and listening intently to any dreaming feedback I might get.

At one point I was on a multi-lane road that was relatively empty when suddenly a large, very loud, white pickup truck came up out of nowhere, fast on my rear, passed me, then cut right in front of me, causing me to brake a little, and shocking me a bit at the aggressiveness of the move. And then I saw: on the back of the truck, right in front of me, was a large white sign with black letters that said: DON’T MOVE HERE. Nothing else—no logos, no images, just the words. I started laughing, and thanked my dreaming for being so obvious, because I could easily have tilted toward making that my choice.

Now I was again at square one—no ideas, just a feeling. Then I had the dream at the top of the chapter, and everything changed.

What to Do with the Unexpected

The dream excerpt at the top of the chapter doesn’t seem life-changing. The inner knowing that each of these images drew out in me, however, was like a bomb going off. I even woke up completely turned around in my bed, feet at headboard. Somehow I knew, deep inside, that the dream meant I would move to France. In the dream I even became lucid and voiced that realization to my dream teacher, saying I knew what it meant but wasn’t sure I had the courage to do it. Upon waking, as I lay in my twisted-up sheets, awake and sweating, I said the same thing out loud to myself. And yet, Myri is in the dream, a friend of mine who moves around the world, always initiated by dreaming and timed with some new publication or enterprise that furthers her development. And as you know by now, Myri, in this dream, is an aspect of me, the dreamer.

The gauntlet was thrown; I knew this move was meant to challenge me. It was a monumental change that was being asked, however, and I wanted to make sure that I was dreaming clearly and not inserting any assumptions into my understanding of it. My dreaming was speaking to me, so I spoke back: I asked for three clear, *waking* confirmations. I sat this question in my mind, holding it gently yet purposefully all throughout the day.

Two days later I woke up with my dog unexpectedly sick. I would have to drive her to the vet in rush-hour traffic. The radio station I always listened to in the car had a joke of giving the weather report with a daily "theme"; for example, one day saying "in Orange County it is 72 degrees today, on Orange Street it is 72, and at Orange Grove Library it is 71." That day, as soon as I turned on the car I heard "At Notre Dame High School it is 70 degrees. . . " Throughout each of the weather reports during the entire forty-five-minute drive I heard all the French-named academies, streets, statues, and other places with French names in Los Angeles. Confirmation Number One was loud and clear!

A couple days later I was jogging in my neighborhood. I lived in a predominantly Korean and Central American neighborhood, with a bilingual Spanish-English elementary school at the end of my block. Jogging along in front of the school I suddenly tripped over something. I caught my balance and turned back to look at it. It was a thick textbook with a picture of the Eiffel Tower on the cover, a happy family waving in front of it, and the title: *Nous Sommes en France* (We are in France). A French-language textbook at a Spanish-English language school. Confirmation Number Two.

Just a day or two after the second confirmation, I went to a friend's boutique clothing store. I needed a dress to take a photo for a dreaming-based project I was working on. While I was in the dressing room, my inner, intuitive voice urged me to tell her about going to France. I hadn't told a single person yet anything about the dream. After a long hesitation, I finally stepped out and told her, omitting the dream part, and simply posing it as an idea that I had been mulling over. She pulled me to the very back of her store where she spread out her computer, pen, and paper on top of a jewelry case. She was training to get a real estate agent license and suggested we work out scenarios for whether I could rent or sell my house, and how I could afford to move. No one else was in the store so we took over the display and got busy.

As we were working, we heard the bell jingle indicating that someone had walked in. We looked up to see a woman marching decisively toward us, all the way to the back of the store, where she asked—in a perfect, native Parisian accent—to see a small necklace in the case we were hunched over. Both of us got chills and our jaws literally dropped. Not only was the Parisian accent a clear confirmation, the event was too strange—there was no way this woman could have seen the necklace, or even the jewelry case, from the street, especially as we were blocking it with our bodies. More important than all of this, though, time suddenly moved very differently, which is one of my personal intuition signals. Every single nerve in my body was on high alert; I physically felt like I had entered a dream while awake.

The French woman moved quickly around the store, trying on the necklace, looking at things. My friend jerked into action and blurted out that I was thinking about moving to France and that we were sorting scenarios at just that moment. She asked the French woman several questions while jabbing me in the ribs to indicate I should be asking her something too. Each question my friend asked, the woman answered, all the while moving and never looking at us, which was also remarkable. It seemed like I had entered a strange bubble, with a silver-pink haze. Finally, I regained movement and said: "I'm trying to figure out if I should move to a big city, like Paris. . . " The woman didn't respond to this, so I continued, ". . . or, if I should live in the countryside, but kind of near a large town I could go to also." At this, the woman stopped for the first time since she had walked into the store. She turned to face me, looked me straight in the eyes, and said "THAT is your dream." Then she abruptly put down the necklace and walked out of the store.

My friend and I stood in stunned silence for several long minutes. She showed me the goosebumps on her arm. I had them, too. I had lived many a dream confirmation in my life, but never anything this overt. My entire body was shaking. Neither of us had mentioned the word dream, and I had purposefully not told my friend that aspect of my process, and still this French woman had called it out explicitly.

"You really have to go there now," my friend said slowly. She was right—confirmation Number Three.

Laying Out the Lessons

The dream story recounted above has a few specific lessons for us to tease out that will help you on your dreaming journey.

The first is **catching the moment**. All dreamwork is embodied, and the practices in this book have suggested ways for turning your focus to your sensing, perceiving self. The more we pay attention to our inner experience, the more we become aware of the inner movements that signal the possibility for evolution and new directions. When we sense this, we can catch the moment, and work with it consciously.

At the same time, catching the moment applies to each step of a dreaming journey. In my own journey, I could easily have been lost in my thoughts, unaware of the radio spouting French names; I could have tripped over the French book and kept going. However, because I sensed change was coming and asked for more information, I was highly attuned to such clues.

A second lesson we can get from my dream story is **walking the dream.** I used this exercise to explore the inner sense I had about moving, as well as during each step of the journey I made to manifest the dream. Once I had my three confirmations and got on board with going to France, I then had to figure out how to get there and where to go. To do this, I set out walking the dream again, sniffing out trails for connections I could make with people who lived there, houses available to rent, and other details that might bring the dream to fruition.

One of the big tools in my dreaming story is **asking a dream for confirmation.** I was exceptionally bold in asking for three waking confirmations, and I have only ever made such an intense request of my dreaming that one time. Confirmations are not to be taken lightly—if we ask, we have to be ready to receive and respond, otherwise we deny our inner knowing and make a rift between our intuitive and willful self. Such a tear compromises our ability to access our truth and introduces doubt. Doubt sets up a disturbing inner conflict; the subsequent distrust in intuition, and the Self, in turn compromises the ability to make further decisions.

Before I asked for the three waking confirmations, I sat quietly and examined myself, making sure I was clear and not in an emotional reaction which might cloud my seeing (I worked the Life Plan), and to be certain that I was ready to act upon whatever answer would arrive. Only then did I ask. If you aren't prepared to follow the response you get from a confirmation, it is better to not ask at all. Instead, keep walking the dream and working the Life Plan, and a path will unfold.

I worked once with a young dreamer facing a decision around graduate school. The international program he settled on had two distinct tracks: each one spent one year in a different country, and both came together in a third country for the second and last year of the program. The program in one European country had the highest reputation and was considered the most difficult to get into. The program in the other country, Norway, came out on paper as the least expensive, especially for international students. The graduate advisor he spoke to said either one would meet his educational needs and suggested the Norway track. This dreamer, however, had his mind set on the more difficult and reputable track.

The dreamer at the time was working for an NGO in an extremely rural part of India. In the days following his phone meeting with the graduate advisor, the word "Norway" came up *five* times in his waking life. No one he knew was considering this same program, or any program in Norway, and he had never mentioned Norway as a country he might be going to. And yet a colleague from his Indian post said, apropos of nothing, "Norway is supposed to be a great place to visit." Three other colleagues stationed in different areas in India mentioned Norway in texts or phone conversations, and while walking in his village he saw it written on a book, with books themselves a rarity where he was. He told me that he was acutely aware of all these mentions and even thought to himself how odd they were, especially given the remote village where he was stationed. And yet, he ignored all of them. He chose the other track.

The choice the dreamer made resulted in two years of extreme difficulty, including advisors who didn't understand what he wanted to research and who subsequently blocked many of his efforts to explore his interests. Interestingly, because both tracks came together in the second year, he was able to compare his experiences with the experiences of friends who had chosen Norway for their initial year. Their experience matched what he had truly been searching for in a graduate program, whereas his did not. He was so disappointed that he changed his career focus altogether after graduation. Reflecting back, he said he was "so set in his mind" on the challenge of the reputable track that he didn't allow an alternative idea to come in, a decision which today he deeply regrets.

This young dreamer had not asked for confirmations for his decision-making as I had in my dreaming journey. And yet, confirmations came. They generally do, in many different forms, because life is not lived in a vacuum; our inner life is reflected in the outer world, and vice versa. The synchronicities and intuitions we discussed in the last chapter are examples of little messages from our dreaming that point us in one direction or another. They show us where energy is vibrating more strongly, between us and the choice, like electrons attracted to the energetic pull of each other. To receive these waking messages, we have to empty ourselves of expectations, assumptions, goals, judgments, and other similar obstructions that crowd our seeing. Keeping an intuition notebook, as you started in the last chapter, will help you to spot these messages, see them accumulate, and—because they are written down—keep you accountable when expectations or doubt start to creep back in.

There's another way that we can receive confirmation, which is by **posing a question to our night dreams**. To do this, write the question in your dream notebook before going to sleep; for example, "tonight I will dream about the college choice that is right for me." Be specific and clear and ask only one question. Not only does that set the stage for your dreaming to be clear in response, it makes deciphering the message easier because it isn't convoluted by numerous requests. Do it for the same question for three nights in a row. Three nights helps us to focus, after which things begin to lose their intensity. If you don't get a clear answer in one of the three, wait a bit—it's not time yet to pose the question.

Keeping track of your dreaming journey—the questions you ask and the intuitions, messages, and synchronicities you receive—is a way of staying clear with yourself. Dreaming journeys move us into new territory, which can bring up all manner of insecurities and resistance. It is very easy, as the young dreamer did above, to dismiss what we really want to do if it butts against what we think others expect us to do. Not only will writing down verify the messages you receive, and help you mark the progress, doing so will develop your dreaming relationship overall and keep you connected to your true inner voice.

By the time I had the dream to go to France, I had already been in a deep relationship with my dreaming for over twenty years. I had logged innumerous dreams and intuition moments in my notebooks, and I had a lot of experience with my dreams giving me messages and then acting on those messages—from rescuing a dog, saying yes to one job and no to another, and buying a home. These experiences had trained me to know when I am clear in receiving dream messages versus when I am crowding in on myself via thoughts, expectations, judgments, fantasy, or wish. Building a practice with the more daily messages of dreaming prepares you for when dreaming poses a big challenge.

My dreaming journey didn't stop with the big message of moving to France; that was only the beginning. Great Dreams continue to unfold as we manifest them in waking life. I still had to *get* to France, and the dreams of how to do so—including where to live—continued to arrive. At each step, I made a point of **expressing my gratitude when receiving messages from my dreaming,** which is the last takeaway from this story so far. Being consciously thankful when our dreaming communicates with us is part of being in dialogue with it, and it strengthens our intention to fuel the changes in our lives.

The dreams that continue to bubble along a dreaming journey not only point us in one direction or another, they bring our attention to inner capabilities that help us to take these next steps. We may be challenged by what a dream is telling us, and the step our dream is daring us to take may be big, but the dream does so knowing that we have what it takes to do it. Because we've dreamed it, we know each of the aspects are a part of us, already. The vision that a dream gives us is a guiding image that we can lean on for the confidence to make it happen.

From Inner Knowing to Outer Doing

Dreaming of moving to a foreign country, where I didn't know anyone or speak the language, was my Mount Everest. And yet, I know that dreams are not whimsical. When I dream Nightmares, I know I am struggling with an emotional reaction, and I know that when I work with the dream to address the Necessity, those struggles resolve. I can trace the Nightmare immediately to what is happening in my waking time. The same is true of Clear Dreams; if they point to a courageous aspect in me, for example, I know I have that capacity somewhere inside me and need to bring it to waking time. These moments, too, I can trace to a waking time situation and apply the dream message to enact change. As any good scientist, I have had multiple experiences of dreaming this way. I don't need to *trust* my dreaming, because I have *experiences* that verify my dreaming. So, even though I was facing a personal Mount Everest in moving to France, I knew it wasn't from nowhere; in me, somewhere, I had what I needed to climb it.

The benefit of a having a dreaming practice, as opposed to occasionally writing down dreams, is that we establish a clear relationship with our inner self and our specific dreaming language. Through experience we learn to distinguish between dreams, make the connections between dreams and waking life, and confirm for ourselves the role of dreams in our personal development. Through this we learn to rely on the inner self and take seriously what our dreams have to say. This experience becomes our advocate for taking the revelations of our dreams and implementing them in our waking life. We take bold steps in life not from outside encouragement (or discouragement, as is often the case), but from our inner, established knowing.

A client of mine, who worked at an established university, had a friend suggest she interview at a different university that was hiring. My client was happy in her current role—as she put it, she "perceived it to be the limit" in terms of salary and scope of work. Something sparked in her at the friend's urging, however, and she put in the application. She was turned down. Months later she received a request from that university to apply for another role. She did, but didn't hear back.

At this point, she dreams she is in a meeting hosted by the university she applied to. There are three round tables, with a white letter face down on each table. She knows it is a job offer and is surprised it came without an interview. She turns over one letter and there is a number on it: \$102,000, signed by a specific woman. The \$102,000 of the dream was higher than her current salary in waking life.

Two weeks after this dream, my client received in waking life an email from the woman who had signed the letter in the dream, asking if she was still interested in the job. That same email laid out that, if taken, the salary range would be \$82–\$90,000. My client replied that she was interested but was aiming for \$102,000. Why? Because she leaned on the message of the dream. As she reported to me, if she hadn't dreamed it, the salary range they offered would have been just fine and she would have accepted it; because of her dream, however, she had the confidence to push. After a few negotiations they settled at \$100,000, a personal financial milestone. Her first day in the office, the dean, whom she hadn't yet met, walked in and told her, "We've been waiting for you." Their partnership has been dynamic, and many positive changes are happening, both in the university and in my client's personal life.

When I talked with my client about this dreaming journey—the seeming dead-end of being rejected for the first post, the endless waiting after applying for the second —she told me that she stayed in the game because her inner knowing had sparked around the university when her friend first suggested it and the dream later confirmed the viability of the choice. Without the dream, she would have settled; because of the dream she had the courage to go for a number that she really wanted to achieve. She sums up the experience like this: "you have to put yourself in a place for magic to happen," and the dream helped her do so.

Intuitions and Great Dreams give us messages that change is both imminent and possible; they don't, however, roll out a red carpet and say that everything will be easy. Things *will* move forward, and sometimes seemingly insurmountable obstacles will miraculously be removed, but we have to put effort toward it—including continuing to address the Necessities of Unresolved Dreams, even Nightmares, that arise as we encounter these obstacles, like my client getting rejected the first time around. Or like having the patience to just keep going. It's that work of keeping the Self clear, untangling energies when they get knotted, and continuing to listen to the dream that puts us in the place for the magic. And we can lean on our intuitive inner knowing and our dreams for the confidence to keep making the effort.

The dream of moving to France, and the three confirmations, resounded particularly loudly for me because I had already recognized the turning of time and sense of imminent change. Even though entertaining the idea immediately created a pile of new challenges—what to do with my house, how would I be able to work—I treated that, too, as a dream and engaged with it as such. Rather than letting it lay inert, wondering if it would come to pass, I curiously explored possibilities. Like a surfer, I began paddling toward the wave I knew would eventually arrive. I was able to catch the moment.

Dreams don't always need confirmations. The dream of my client and the new job, and the dream of the woman with the red motorboat we met in Chapter One, were clear enough to each of them right away. Often, we sense something we are meant to be doing, but ignore it, like the young dreamer who ignored the signs that pointed him to the Norway track. Most of the time, it isn't confirmation that is needed, but the courage to act on our inner knowing. That, and getting ourselves in a place for the magic to happen.

If we take the challenge of dreams, explore them, and push to move them forward they respond back. Like the client who had the initial intuition, then later—after the rejection—had the dream signaling the offer, our dreaming self will continue to provide little stepping stones to guide us along the way. My French journey was no different.

I said yes to France, but it's a big country—where did I need to go? I dreamed the answer, months into the work of trying to organize a visa. In this dream I see only a map of the country, with only one city name next to a single red dot. Around that dot is a red circle. I understand that in that city, or the countryside within the circle around it, is where I need to live. Shortly after dreaming this, I get a call from a friend of a friend. He has a cousin with an apartment I can rent—the missing piece for getting my visa. I might not like the area, he tells me, but I can use it as a base to at least get me in the country. I ask for the address and, as you expected, it's right in the circle. Not only did it resolve a big hurdle in my getting to France, it anticipated and resolved another one before it ever came up: making friends. The cousin with the apartment is today one of my closest.

It may seem strange that dreams can be so anticipatory. In the last chapter about intuition, we looked at how we are part of an interconnected web. The ancient science of dreaming sees that web as containing all possibility. As we make choices in our life, walking forward in our journey, we tug on different strands of this web, creating vibrations and resonances like plucking a string on a violin. Which string, and how we pluck it, causes other strands to vibrate, connecting other people and events, and determining the possibilities we encounter. We think we are doing this in a linear way, one step in front of the other, but in dream, time is all-at-once, a little like the inner knowing of an intuition. Through dream we can peek into this larger view of possibility, looking far into the web. When we do that, we bring new elements into our lives, very much like introducing new evolutionary traits, that transform us on deep levels. Because the web is not static, but constantly responding to these changes, we then shift the entire lot of possibility—for us, and for others. But only if we make it manifest.

There are many dreams that float through our lives, but acting on a dream to bring it from something envisioned to something lived is the real work of dreaming. When we start to actively manifest the dream messages of our lives—whether it be to shift a Nightmare from unresolved to resolved, or to take a big step to change jobs, career, or country—we move from being just dreamers to become the Great Dreamers of our lives. Being a Great Dreamer, we change not only our own lives, but also the lives of others. In the next and final chapter of our book we look at exactly that: the impact of our dreaming.

CHAPTER ELEVEN

Change Your Dreams, Change the World—The Impact of Your Dreaming

"I sit on the ground, my back against a tree. As I breathe, so does it. My exhale it inhales; its exhale I inhale. We breathe together, in harmony. For a moment, I become the tree—rooting deep down into the earth and at the same time stretching tall and sending branches wide. Then I am sitting again, separate, and breathing with it. I stand up, turn, and look at the tree—now it is bathed in golden light, immensely tall, with a thick crown and golden apples. Golden birds fly in and among the fruits. I see I am dressed like an old-fashioned traveler, with sturdy brown boots and a stick over my shoulder with a red scarf tied on the end to hold my belongings. I feel the tree wants me to open the scarf, and when I do countless golden seeds spill out. I understand I am to be like the Johnny Appleseed of dreams, traveling the world and planting the dream seeds wherever I go. I gather up the seeds, put the stick over my shoulder, and take my first step."

—DREAMER

How many things can you imagine a circle to be? A circle that provokes nearly endless possibilities, or a circle that is seen as just a circle?

The challenge posed in the introduction to this book invited you to see just how high the stakes are when we decide whether or not to choose to open our imaginations to seeing possibilities and solutions beyond the literal, the familiar, and what we assume or expect. As individuals it means the difference between repeating patterns or living freely; between following habits or offering original contributions. Society is composed of individuals, so opening our imaginations also means the difference of whether we, as a human community, consign ourselves to repeating the patterns of history, or catapult ourselves to new ways of collaborating to solve our shared, global problems.

The eight-year-old looking at a circle will see many things, like the steering wheel of a racecar, the porthole of a submarine, or the entrance to a dragon's lair. It's not just unique things they see, what they envision is elaborate and active. The racecar, submarine, and dragon's lair come with scenarios and invitations of new places the image can take them. Adults, on the other hand, see only the obvious circle, or black circle on a white page.[1] Flat, literal, unelaborate, and with no invitation to take the question further.

As I mentioned at the beginning of this book, creativity scores in America have been sharply declining,[2] with companies like IBM[3] and Adobe[4] desperately looking to hire creative individuals, yet drawing blanks in their searches.[5]

The eight-year-olds who see in a simple circle ninety different things are, in many ways, better equipped to tackle the complex problems we face today as a society than adults hired to solve them. These declining creative skills include the ability to find the essence of a problem, think critically, and produce ideas—all essential ingredients if we want to tackle things like pandemics, energy needs, and living in a renewable balance with our planet. The decision to try and tackle problems is itself a problem these days; even the motivation to be creative has declined.

Losing these skills has dire ramifications. I cited creativity researcher Mark Runco's experiments where college students are asked to list all problems that would keep them from graduating, then choose one of those items and come up with as many solutions for it as possible. The correlation between suicidal ideation and students who were unable to find solutions to the problems they listed—even when controlling for pre-existing levels of depression and anxiety—is high.[6] The despair of not being able to see beyond a problem by imagining something different halts the road of an individual's life and rings alarm bells for us as a society.

We dreamers have seen standstill before—feeling frozen in dreams, unable to move; getting off the train before arriving at the destination. We've seen blocks like cardboard boxes, and overwhelming anxiety in cars racing toward gaping holes. We've seen the tendency to step out of dances, and step away from love. More importantly, we've seen all of these transformed, freeing both the inner image to imagine something different and the dreamer to move and create differently in their waking lives.

Creativity and dreaming are intimately linked. Each of the steps and components described in this book for how to work with dreams directly cultivates creativity, building creative strengths like problem-identifying and perspective-taking, and synthesizing different pieces of information to create new outputs. Developing a relationship with our dreams heightens perception, increases imagination and fluency of ideas, and fosters our ability to articulate numerous strands of thought and the meaning we draw from them. We learn to think critically when we work with dreams, noticing patterns and anticipating their possible outcomes, and assigning best fit to ideas by recognizing both Necessities and potentials.

Finally, ideas prompt ideas—the never-ending new images and perspectives of dreams keep our imaginations original and active.

The most practical thing we can do today is learn how to dream again. When we take the dreams and visions of our inner self and make them our waking reality, we impact not only our own life, but also the lives of all around us—even society as a whole.

This book has worked to return you to your own inner dreaming and imagination, to give you tools to resolve your personal emotional contradictions and inner constraints, and to stretch yourself to access and utilize more of what you are capable of. To imagine yourself, your families, and your world differently.

In the last chapter we looked at dreamers who used their Great Dreams to move to new jobs (even countries) and write new chapters in their life story. All of us have this capacity. In this chapter we will look at how each of us can be Great Dreamers and bring transformation to a global scale.

Dreaming and Creativity

Usually, you can put a group of young kids together, like we do at the International Institute for Dreaming and Imagery® DYW Kids® program, where we teach dreaming and intuition skills to young dreamers, and they get excited about figuring things out. Whether it is turning ordinary trash bags into costumes (because someone forgot to bring the supplies) or creating an entire musical based on confronting monsters and addressing the Necessity, their minds are electric with nonstop ideas. Put a group of teenagers together and they need to be coaxed a little. Get in a room with a group of professional adults and the energy is flat. The tendency is to sit and wait for someone else to speak, and then hitch comments onto theirs—"like James just said, I. . . "

I teach in numerous venues, from leadership development programs in organizations to classes taught at the Institute. The difference between a group of adults who don't yet have a relationship to their dreams and a group of adults who do is profound. Like the young kids, the adult dreamers pop with ideas, thinking far beyond the literal, reaching a place of deep imagination that is at once addressing the question or task I posed, as well as connecting it to how it will affect multiple other areas that are at first glance unconnected. They are also comfortable having unique thoughts, never parroting what has already been said. Comments are built upon or taken in new directions.

One of the exercises I start with to teach leaders is to show a series of images and have the leaders describe what they see. Within three responses people usually settle into groupthink. A story gets formed around what they presume to be the subject of the image, even though the instruction is to simply give a visual description. That story, once formed, remains unchallenged even in a large class of twenty-five participants.

Watching how quickly a pattern gets formed in this way gives us a window into why companies begin with the energy of a new idea and quickly stagnate, why organizations lose track of their mission and turn their focus toward maintaining the organization, and why academic disciplines circle around and perpetuate established ideas while stifling research in new theories and inquiries.

Dreamers are the natural antidote to this organizational inertia. Dreaming develops the ability to move out of parroting, story-making, and groupthink, the nefarious ingredients that stymie most groups. Not only do dreamers have the courage to access their imagination, where they know they will find infinite ideas, they have the courage to contribute that unique way of seeing to others. This includes dreamers of all ages, from young kids to teens to adults.

A group of individuals thinking for themselves raises fears of anarchy for some—how can teams be built with everyone having their own ideas about how to do things? Remember that dreaming develops empathy—it is by having so many unique ideas that dreamers are able to appreciate and hold space for the ideas of others. Knowing that each person contains a ceaseless source of ideas inside themselves means other people's ideas are not threatening. Dreamers come equipped with the skills of perspective-taking and emotional regulation. This makes dreamers able to see the big picture, as well as the specific, making them natural contributors and collaborators working together for a shared vision.

Creativity researcher Ruth Richards writes that creativity in groups and work is often "underrecognized, underdeveloped, and underrewarded."[7] Time, or the lack thereof, is one of the biggest threats that keeps us from accessing our creativity—from not spending time exploring our own creativity, to not taking time to hear the ideas of others.[8] New ideas inherently disrupt the status quo. For the nondreamer this opening-out of structures is destabilizing. It spells cognitive overload in an already overloaded, demanding workspace. It feels like just getting the pieces of a fragile puzzle in place only to have someone want to take it apart again. The knee-jerk response is to be conservative with change, even if the new ideas may ultimately make things smoother and more efficient, or even innovative.

Establishing a dreaming practice, that simple little homework in Chapter One, is the first step for turning the tide on the creativity crisis. One of the many skills this builds is the ability to be flexible around change. Dream, and we slip into a different world, with its own completely different logic. It is a world we fully immerse ourselves in, meeting whatever challenges arise in this unique scenario, just as they appear, without losing time comparing it to how different it is from what's familiar. Wake, and we are yet again in a new world. Dream again, and we are immersed in yet another world. Doing this with awareness night after night creates a skill for navigating shifting scenarios, rules, structures, and logic. At work, for example, a team of dreamers gets energized about going back to the drawing board. The dreaming manager knows the value of fresh ideas and takes time to explore team member insights. The fragile puzzle-structures of projects or organizations can be taken apart, and reconfigured, without fear.

Our first go-to in approaching challenge and decision is what we already know and expect. These ready reactions come early in the neurosynaptic chain, tend toward pattern and convention, and are unoriginal. Breakthroughs and original ideas, on the other hand, operate along the farthest ends of the associative neuropathway.[9] These loose associations put things together in ways we wouldn't normally expect—the very definition of innovation.

Think back to some of your most memorable dreams; often, it is the "weirdest" of elements that resonate the most—giant supernovas in the shape of lions, the couch-turned-masked-man we encountered, or the obsidian egg-ring that becomes a suspended crystalline structure. The new ideas of dream are part of the generative, creative process. They work at the farthest ends of our associative neuropathways, drawing from known experience and yet providing completely new scenarios and characters for which we have no prior reference.[10] The provocation of surprise in seeing these images engages the free, spontaneous imagination, prompting the origination of new ideas. While we lay snuggled in the sheets exploring all the possible meanings, associations, and memories elicited by these strange images, we are actively engaging multiple divergent thinking skills. If we develop a relationship with our dreams, we not only become party to this flow of new ideas every night—thinking in this way while awake becomes second nature. Bringing these skills to the workplace, we become catalysts for more engaging and fruitful ideation sessions.

Training ourselves to engage with strange images and ideas also develops the creative skills of openness and curiosity. Unless we are motivated, we hang out in the early parts of the neurosynaptic chain, resorting to routine, assumption, and what's worked before.[11] It's worse when we've invested in an area of knowledge or expertise; as "subject matter experts" we work to protect that investment rather than "risk" being exposed to new and perhaps contradicting information,[12] especially ones that would send us back to square one. Engaging in a dreaming practice, however, frees us to innovate; instead of subject matter experts we become creative experts, playing with a wide range of information that catapults our knowledge areas to new grounds. This flexibility frees us as individuals to renew and reinvent our personal and professional lives through time and change. An organization composed of such individual dreamers is resilient and resourceful in the face of shifting marketplaces and societal needs.

The tendency to hold fast to known structures and assumptions, and to ignore the original, is found in every field, even in science, the supposed domain of new ideas. The default network, where dreaming and creativity is centered, took *forty years* to be treated seriously in the scientific community after the initial bit of data was found suggesting its existence.[13] It first emerged in studies recording brain activity when participants were engaged in a task like adding up a series of numbers. The researchers assumed that the brain would jolt into action during the task and then revert to a nonactive rest state once the task was completed. However, in study after study, they found that this so-called "rest" state was actually *more* active. Still, they dismissed it. Despite the fact that a hard-to-ignore accumulation of research showed that the brain becomes more active "at rest" than when engaged in a goal-directed, rational, and computational task, the *idea* that the brain was invested in imagining, and that cognition included other things like emotion, imagery, and memory, remained inconceivable.

These activities literally lay hidden in plain sight, unseen by researchers blinded by their own expectations and assumptions of how the brain works and how "thinking" is defined. Even after the data reached an indisputable height, there continued a trend in science journals to not report on or explore the meaning of the findings because it seemed too preposterous. Finally, after a few bold publications, researchers began to reimagine brain cognition. And I use that word "imagine" intentionally.

The story of the default network is about the tendency to dismiss that which doesn't immediately fit into known paradigms, to toss aside the things which we don't immediately understand or for which we don't immediately perceive a use. We can only imagine how many breakthrough discoveries have been passed over, unseen.

This story doesn't belong to science alone. It is perhaps the greatest limiting factor when it comes to individuals moving beyond pattern to explore the mystery of possibility in their own lives. Invested in our own Presenting "I", we hold fast to certain assumptions about self, family, career, and other structures we've constructed, rather than curiously exploring different perspectives and new ideas. We are the "subject matter experts" of the self, which often just means overfamiliarity with pattern. Sometimes positive ways of seeing ourselves (e.g., "I am courageous", "I have something original to contribute", "I am capable of being loved and loving others", or "I can move past failure") feel to us like the most outlandish ideas we harbor about ourselves. To bring these to waking realities, we must be iconoclasts, smashing fixed ideas, and stretching into new ways of being, something that dreams help us to do. The more we relax our hold on our own personal assumptions, the more potentials we access within ourselves to bring to our own lives, our families, and the communal table.

We don't control what we see in dreams. They operate in the most free and unrestrained of our conscious states. We saw in the last chapter how, in dream, we can look far into the web of possibility that connects us all. We are able to do that because the aspects of our neurological processing that typically judge and limit what we perceive are shut down in dream.[14] Without that bouncer at the door, we have access to a different space of ideas, experience, and knowing, including, perhaps the most audacious knowing of all, that of "I can."

The emotions we feel in seeing and interacting with dream images in this state are very real. That sense of embodiment is key because it means that we stay anchored to a sense of self even as the definitions of that self may be altered in the dream.[15] In wake I may be timid, but in dream I may take my place on the diplomatic stage, sharing a critical perspective on lawmaking. The *feeling* of being able to voice that point of view to others is real, making it possible to then bring it into waking time and manifest it tangibly. This is one way that dreams distinguish themselves from fantasy. It is their proof text for being treated with absolute seriousness.

Dreams further distinguish themselves from fantasy because of their inherent meaningfulness. The outrageous new ideas they propose are directly applicable, because they are aspects of the self. This means that the new ideas of dream can be received in sleep rather than defended against if they counter what we know and expect in waking time. The one who waits for the right partner, or opens the door to the salsa music, or jumps in the river despite the lack of a safety ring—these aspects we've seen before are part of dream's coherent restructuring of experience.[16] The Presenting "I" interacts with them directly, in various ways, without asking why they showed up. This interaction, literally, opens our minds to other possibilities. The question is: Can we stay open to this when we wake up and bring our most expanded self to contribute to society as a whole?

Creativity researcher Mark Runco puts it this way: Creativity "boils down to a kind of freedom of thought."[17] We can shut down our dreams as implausible, as the forty years of scientists did around the default network. If, however, we wake up and continue to work with the dream as we've done in this book, taking the promptings of our dreams as material to consciously explore, then we begin the work of manifesting the potential of dream to reality. If we are willing to allow ourselves to see possibility in our own lives, we become the conscious creators of it. If we are willing to see the possibility present in our world, we become conscious collaborators with it.

The method taught in this book gives us a means for continuing the free play of ideas presented in dreams once we are awake. Take the four levels of dreams, for example. Working through them we discover multiple perspectives and meanings, including imaginatively experiencing the point of view of the many other characters who are present, moving us beyond one static view to new interpretations. The same four levels, and the work of finding the Necessity, use the creative strengths of pattern recognition and problem-finding,[18] both related to discovering and articulating new questions.[19] Questions, if we don't shut them down, always take us farther. They crack open the doors of what we expect, making way for a stream of new ideas.

Dreams are famously the catalyst for invention, literature, and other society-changing ideas. Elias Howe, the inventor of the modern sewing machine, for example, met repeated failure attempting to imitate the hand sewing method used by his wife until he had a dream of cannibals carrying him off to be executed. He noticed in the dream that they carried spears that had holes in the tip. Upon waking reflection, it was this unexpected placement of the hole—in the tip and not the end, as hand sewing needles are made—that was the breakthrough that resolved his design issues.[20] Because he didn't dismiss the dream, but instead experimented with it, he—along with society as a whole—advanced.

Let's not forget Einstein. The theory of relativity came to him in a dream in which he told a farmer about cows surrounded by a fence. He was on one side, the farmer on the other, and he realized the farmer saw the scene differently than him.[21] This is a perfect example of how dreams work with new perspectives, and the new perspective in this dream blasted open society-shifting ideas of relativity, subjectivity, and the very idea of mutability within our natural world, effectively returning humans to co-creators in the earth system in which we live, rather than mute recipients of an experience determined solely by rigid, natural laws. In other words, his dream brought all of us back to dreaming.

These kinds of problem-solving insights don't have to wait for night dreams, though. As you've learned in this book, we can access the space of spontaneous imagination while awake. General Electric, attempting to resolve an issue with the design of their dishwashers using their engineers' usual methods, repeatedly hit blocks until they were challenged to solve the problem using only imaginary animal parts. A dishwasher imagined as elephant trunks and parrot beaks suddenly brought the solution to light.[22]

Highly creative people show high levels of intrinsic motivation, which plays out in multiple ways including an openness to experience as well as energy put toward elaborating on ideas and possibilities.[23] They continue to engage with what-ifs, while others simply remain in the what-is. The intrinsic motivation to play with ideas and continue to elaborate upon them—even those that imply breaking apart knowledge structures—is equally a hallmark of dreamers.

To the dreamer, the world is not fixed, but an in-process experience where both Self and structures are iterative and mutable. The structures, forms, and perspectives that appear in one dream one night, and are reconfigured with wholly new presentations the next, create such a worldview.

This very aspect of dreaming is what Harvard researcher David Kahn sees as the neurological origin of self-concept.[24] In his view, the creation of novel, coherent scenarios in dreams are part of a self-organizing process our system undergoes in response to challenges in our waking environment. We experience things we otherwise wouldn't be able to in waking time, thus expanding the waking self; structures are dismantled, and a new structure is created that is more complex than the sum of its parts. "Who I am," in other words, is not a fixed idea, but one that is ever evolving, with dream being the body's natural mechanism for ensuring this adaptive ability.

The subjectivity of dreams is important because it ensures that the self-organized being is fully expressive of its individuality. Michel Jouvet, the neuroscientist and dream researcher we met in Chapter One, hypothesizes that neural mechanisms active in REM sleep preserve individuality even on a genetic basis, allowing the individual to emerge beyond the constraints of socialization—one of the great sources of pattern in our lives—thus making that emergence an important aspect of human evolution as a whole.[25]

The more we bring our own unique self into being, the more we shift the whole, bringing a fresh flow of new possibility to existing patterns. The web shifts, and new strands are plucked, making possible the emergence of infinite other ways of seeing our world. New possibilities appear, and entire systems shift.

Dreaming and Transformation

How do we imagine the Self?

The dream at the top of the chapter is a dream of mine. It is one of many dreams I've had over the years about teaching this dreamwork to others. Bringing dreams from revelation to action—confronting challenges and using dreams to overcome them—has shaped me into the person I am today. Ultimately, dreams are a path to self-becoming.

Dreams surprise us, in part, because they override waking limitations and preoccupations to show us what we aren't seeing in ourselves. The healing mechanism of dreams is the breaking down of patterns, and the dismantling of structures, that allows for the big idea of who we really are to come to the fore. Because dreams are a phenomenon that arises from within the Self, the question we ask of dreams "what does that mean" is, automatically, "what does that mean for me?" The unexpected thus becomes possibility, prompting the cognitive restructuring of what we once thought were limitations to what we might, now, be capable of.

Frozen, stuck, separated from love—we know from cognitive psychology and neuroscience, as well as the ancient science of dreaming, that the images in our body-mind are direct commands to the body-system;[26] if we see stuck, we *are* stuck. As long as the image persists, so, too, does that blocked state of waking action. To change that, we have to change the image. Modern science is beginning to understand this, too, but they lack a way for how to do it. This is something that the ancient science of dreaming uniquely brings to the table: a means for operationalizing how we access and work with the images of our experience. Stuck can become unstuck and blocks can be jumped over, gone around, or removed.

The ultimate Great Dream is the Dream of Self. We see it in momentary flickers, accessing it in the daily images and nightly dreams that compel us to bring it into being, bit by bit, along our life walk. To do that, though, we have to take our dreams seriously—and playfully—exercising our innate creativity toward realizing their promptings. In the last chapter we saw that the Great Dreamers of the world are the ones who listen to their dreams and do something with them in waking life to bring the potential to actual.

Each time we access our dreams, and use them to shift our waking experience, we impact not only our own life, but the lives of those around us—even those we don't know. Like one great body, the world depends on the unique contributions of each individual. Heart, lungs, kidneys, and liver each rely on the fully functioning other in their interconnected system; likewise, the world body awaits the specific uniqueness of each individual—many individual dreams as aspects of the one Great Dream of humanity.

We are changed by our dreams and act upon that change in the world.[27] All the thousand touchpoints one individual encounters in a day aggregate, shifting the collective. In the same way that replacing a single thread with a differently colored one alters the pattern of a large tapestry, one individual transformation shifts the communal dream, contributing to systems-wide change.[28]

Experiences like those in Great Dreams, like nothing we've ever experienced before, change our way of being and relating to the world. They are the dreams that contain the insights needed to solve the problems of our own era. Can anyone imagine, amid today's apocalyptic headlines, a verdant, abundant world where all life—human and animal—has the ability to flourish? I can, only because I've dreamed it. It's the power of dreaming that wakes us up to the positive good we can grow, and to envision the highest potential for humanity as a whole.

Dreams in history gave rise to the invention of tools, healing processes, and judicial and societal structures.[29] Dreams today continue to alter the trajectory of both individual lives and, through them, humankind. Dreams have figured in the sciences—from the already-mentioned sewing machine to the shape of the benzene ring, the periodic table of elements, Niels Bohr's structure of the atom, and insulin as a medicine for diabetes. The proof that nerves use chemicals to transmit signals which won Sir Henry Dale and Otto Loewi the Nobel Prize in Medicine in 1936 came from a dream, as did thousands of the mathematical theorems of Srinivasa Ramanujan, who was featured in the movie *The Man Who Knew Infinity*. Dreams have contributed to the arts, including the song "Yesterday," by Paul McCartney for the Beatles, the book *Twilight*, the song "Satisfaction" by Keith Richards for the Rolling Stones, the ending of Handel's *Messiah*, and many of Beethoven's works, including pieces he wrote for instruments not yet invented.[30] Ideas build upon each other. The more we bring the ideas of our dreams into the collective, the more the collective dreams.

This book set out to argue four main points, the first of which is that we dream all the time, night as well as day. Research from the default network provides evidence for this case from a physical perspective.

Beyond neurological phenomenon, however, is the perspective of the ancient science of dreaming that looks at life as being more than what is seen on the surface. When we peer at waking life through the four levels of dreams, we perceive a world that is malleable. No longer fixed, waking life becomes a dream where patterns can be shifted, new perspectives imagined and brought forth, and where Necessities can be identified and solved, sending us on entirely new trajectories. Becoming conscious to this means we have the ability to change entire structures and do so with creativity and resourcefulness.

Two more points made in this book are that the material of dreams is meaningful and that dreams are rife with transformative potential. Not at all whimsical, dreams orient us to where we are physically, emotionally, mentally, and spiritually in our present tense. These two points become clear by understanding that we form inner images by the experiences we live and that by working with our dreams and discovering how they relate to our waking life, we begin speaking the visual language of images.

Dream's ability to orient us as individuals applies equally to entire communities. When we apply the four levels of dream, and the kinds of dreams, to waking life on a social scale we find it, too, mirrors back to us what can be called the communal dream, reflective of our communal experience. Like individual dreams, viewing waking life this way also presents new possibilities, as well as revealing blocks. And, like individual dreams, if we look at it through dreamer's eyes, it provides the means for transforming them.

We find the communal dream by looking at the external images that perpetuate in our cultures, listening to the stories we tell, and moving through these "dream artifacts" in the same way we work through the four levels of an individual dream—from story to finding patterns, and then searching for the deeper meaning. We wait for a question to arise and pose it. The communal dream can be a Nightmare or Great Dream; unresolved or resolved. If unresolved, the Necessity can be identified and responded to. If the Necessity is not responded to, however, just like with an individual dream, the communal dream remains unresolved, nonharmonious, and in conflict.

Communal dreams are composed of the millions of individuals acting out their own individual dreams; the products we make carry the resonances of the images we hold inside. The blocked individual develops belief systems that are propagated, from advice given to a friend, to the theories taught in a classroom, to the books that are written, to the governments we elect.

Systems can't change when they are constructed by individuals who are curtailing their natural creative expression, bending to societal and familial pressures, or restraining their thoughts and intellectual contributions for fear of nonconformity or retribution. We don't create when stopped by fear or anger. Being able to stop speeding cars heading toward a crash, open the door to intimacy and salsa music, jump into the flow, and get back on the train to get to center frees entangled energies that are now able to do ever bigger work, like healing our families, communities, and organizations. The courage to unblock leads to courage to come forward with a new idea, offer a contrary position, to speak truth to a lie, to face a conflict and resolve it, to seek peace when others pursue anger. Unblocked, our unique talents and abilities express themselves, enriching the communal dream, and inspiring others.

Each of us is capable of being an agent of change. We can address the Necessities of our own individual dreams, and we can respond to the Necessities of the communal dream. Both require a conscious, responsive relationship with our dreaming. The individual dreamer who faces their blocks and resolves them fashions themselves into a clear vessel, able to receive Great Dreams—to enter the place of true envisioning, far beyond problem-solving. The communal dream self-perpetuates until it is consciously engaged with and reenvisioned. By Great Dreaming we stretch beyond our perceived limitations, in ways that no daytime "brainstorming" or creative session can create. Through Great Dreams we are able to truly imagine our world differently. We expand, and our view of the world expands with us.

In times past, communities used to dream together and talk about their dreams as a group. These dream time moments brought people together to create together. The big ideas of dreams became the big ideas of their waking life. Today we, as a whole system, have a question about our planet. What is the image we collectively hold for ourselves, our role in it, and our future? How would the communal dream shift with not one, but many dreamers bringing their Great Dreams forward, inspiring us to look again, to see it differently, to engage and respond from a place of possibility?

The world needs dreamers and the new images of all that is possible. Working to face our personal Nightmares, resolve our conflicts, and address the Necessities of our dreams creates Great Dreamers. The communal dream shifts, and systems change. We move, together, from dreaming a communal Nightmare to ever-clearer dreams of the unfolding human potential. The keys to our transformation, in both the Self and humanity as a whole, are in the secret mind of dreaming.

Notes

Introduction

1. Kyung Hee Kim, "The Creativity Crisis: The Decrease in Creative Thinking Scores on the Torrance Tests of Creative Thinking," *Creativity Research Journal* 23, no. 4 (2011): 285—295, https://www.doi.org/10.1080/10400419.2011.627805.

2. Ahmed M. Abdulla and Bonnie Cramond, "After Six Decades of Systematic Study of Creativity: What Do Teachers Need to Know About What It Is and How It Is Measured?" *Roeper Review* 39, no. 1 (2017): 9—23, https://doi.org/10.1080/02783193.2016.1247398; Po Bronson and Ashley Merryman, "The Creativity Crisis," *Newsweek*, accessed 2017, http://www.newsweek.com/creativity-crisis-74665; Sue Shellenbarger, "A Box? Or a Spaceship? What Makes Kids Creative?" *Wall Street Journal*, updated 2010, https://www.wsj.com/articles/SB10001424052748704694004576019462107929014.

3. Ruth Richards, "Introduction," in *Everyday Creativity and New Views of Human Nature: Psychological, Social, and Spiritual Perspectives* (American Psychology Association, 2007).

4. "World Economic Forum, Future of Jobs Report," accessed January 2024, at https://www.weforum.org/publications/the-future-of-jobs-report-2023/digest/.

5. Bronson and Merryman, "The Creativity Crisis."

6. Mark Andrews, "Creative skills and digital literacy: Equipping the next generation for success," *Adobe* (blog), September 29, 2021, https://blog.adobe.com/en/publish/2021/09/29/equipping-the-next-generation-with-creative-skills-and-digital-literacy.

7. "The Bloomberg Recruiter Report: Job Skills Companies Want But Can't Get," *Bloomberg* (blog), accessed January 2023, at https://www.bloomberg.com/graphics/2015-job-skills-report/.

8. Kim, "The Creativity Crisis: The Decrease in Creative Thinking Scores on the Torrance Tests of Creative Thinking."

9. Bronson and Merryman, "The Creativity Crisis."

10. G. William Domhoff and Kieran C.R. Fox, "Dreaming and the default network: A review, synthesis, and counterintuitive research proposal," *Consciousness and Cognition* 33 (2015): 342—353, https://pubmed.ncbi.nlm.nih.gov/25723600/; Patrick McNamara, *The Neuroscience of Sleep and Dreams* (Cambridge University Press, 2019).

11. McNamara, *The Neuroscience of Sleep and Dreams.*

12. Richards, *Everyday Creativity and New Views of Human Nature: Psychological, Social, and Spiritual Perspectives.*

13. Kim, "The Creativity Crisis: The Decrease in Creative Thinking Scores on the Torrance Tests of Creative Thinking."

14. Ibid.

15. Ibid.

16. Hailie Brophy, Joanne Olson, and Pauline Paul, "Eco-anxiety in youth: An integrative literature review," *Int J Mental Health Nurs.* 32 (2023): 633—661, https://pubmed.ncbi.nlm.nih.gov/36582129/.

17. McNamara, *The Neuroscience of Sleep and Dreams.*

18. Kim, "The Creativity Crisis: The Decrease in Creative Thinking Scores on the Torrance Tests of Creative Thinking"; Richards, *Everyday Creativity and New Views of Human Nature: Psychological, Social, and Spiritual Perspectives*; Mark A. Runco, "Meta-Creativity: Being Creative About Creativity," *Creativity Research Journal* 27, no. 3 (2015): 295—298, https://doi.org/10.1080/10400419.2015.1065134; Mark A. Runco, "Commentary: Overview of Developmental Perspectives on Creativity and the Realization of Potential," in *Perspectives on Creativity Development*, ed. Baptiste Barbot (Wiley Periodicals, 2016), 97–109.

19. See, for example: Roger E. Beaty, Mathias Benedek, Scott Barry Kaufman, and Paul J. Silvia, "Default and Executive Network Coupling Supports Creative Idea Production," *Scientific Reports* 5, no. 10964 (2015): https://doi.org/10.1038/srep10964; Kelly Bulkeley, "Dreaming is imaginative play in sleep: A theory of the function of dreams," *American Psychological Association: Dreaming*, 29, no. 1 (2019): 1—29; Domhoff and Fox, "Dreaming and the default network: A review, synthesis, and counterintuitive research proposal"; McNamara, *The Neuroscience of Sleep and Dreams*.

20. Richards, *Everyday Creativity and New Views of Human Nature: Psychological, Social, and Spiritual Perspectives*.

21. McNamara, *The Neuroscience of Sleep and Dreams*.

22. Kelly Bulkeley, *Big Dreams: The Science of Dreaming and the Origins of Religion* (Oxford University Press, 2016); McNamara, *The Neuroscience of Sleep and Dreams*.

23. Malidoma Patrice Somé, "A Healing Relationship with the Ancestors," *Jung Platform*, https://jungplatform.com/store/a-healing-relationship-with-the-ancestors.

24. Bulkeley, *Big Dreams: The Science of Dreaming and the Origins of Religion*.

25. Kim, "The Creativity Crisis: The Decrease in Creative Thinking Scores on the Torrance Tests of Creative Thinking."

26. Larry Page, "University of Michigan Commencement Address, Spring 2009," accessed November 2024, at https://www.youtube.com/watch?v=qFb2rvmrahc&t=12s.

27. Elisa Roland, "13 World-Changing Ideas That Came from Dreams (Literally),"*Reader's Digest online*, accessed December 2021, at https://www.rd.com/list/ideas-that-came-from-dreams/.

Chapter One

1. Rav Chisda, *Tractate Berachos* (Schottenstein Edition, 1997), 55a (47).

2. McNamara, *The Neuroscience of Sleep and Dreams*.

3. Ibid.

4. Cited in Bulkeley, *Big Dreams: The Science of Dreaming and the Origins of Religion*.

5. Michel Jouvet, *The Paradox of Sleep: The Story of Dreaming*, trans. Laurence Garey (The MIT Press, 1999), 27.

6. McNamara, *The Neuroscience of Sleep and Dreams*.

7. Ibid.

8. Throughout this book I refer to the default network and executive networks. My primary source material are the reviews: Jessica R. Andrews-Hanna, "The Brain's Default Network and Its Adaptive Role in Internal Mentation," *Neuroscientist* 18 (2012): 251, https://doi.org/10.1177/1073858411403316; Jessica R. Andrews-Hanna, "The default network and self-generated thought: component processes, dynamic control, and clinical relevance," *Annals of the New York Academy of Sciences* (2014): 1—24, https://doi.org/10.1111/nyas.12360; Randy L. Buckner, Jessica R. Andrews-Hanna, and Daniel L. Schachter, "The Brain's Default Network: Anatomy, Function, and Relevance to Disease," *Annals of the New*

York Academy of Sciences, 1124 (2008): 1–38, https://doi.org/10.1196/annals.1440.011.

9. Beaty, Benedek, and Kaufman, "Default and Executive Network Coupling Supports Creative Idea Production."

10. G. William Dalhoff, *The Emergence of Dreaming: Mind-Wandering, Embodied Simulation, and the Default Network* (Oxford University Press, 2018).

11. Mary Helen Immordino-Yang, Joanna A. Christodoulou, and Vanessa Singh, "Rest Is Not Idleness: Implications of the Brain's Default Mode for Human Development and Education," *Perspectives on Psychological Science* 7, no. 4 (2012): 352—364, https://doi.org/10.1177/1745691612447308.

12. Ibid.

13. Josie E. Malinowski and Caroline L. Horton, "Metaphor and hyperassociativity: the imagination mechanisms behind emotion assimilation in sleep and dreaming," *Front. Psychol.* 6 (2015): 1132, https://doi.org/10.3389/fpsyg.2015.01132.

14. Ernest Hartmann, "The Nature and Functions of Dreaming," in *The New Science of Dreaming: Volume 3, Cultural and Theoretical Perspectives*, eds. Deirdre Barrett and Patrick McNamara (Praeger Publishers/Greenwood Publishing Group, 2007).

15. "1 in 3 adults don't get enough sleep," *Centers for Disease Control and Prevention*, accessed December 2021, at https://archive.cdc.gov/www_cdc_gov/media/releases/2016/p0215-enough-sleep.html; McNamara, *The Neuroscience of Sleep and Dreams.*

16. McNamara, *The Neuroscience of Sleep and Dreams.*

17. John Read, *From Alchemy to Chemistry* (Dover Publications, 1995).

18. cited in Bulkeley, *Big Dreams: The Science of Dreaming and the Origins of Religion.*

19. McNamara, *The Neuroscience of Sleep and Dreams.*

20. See, for example: Kelly Bulkeley, "Dreaming is imaginative play in sleep: A theory of the function of dreams," *Dreaming* 29, no. 1 (2019): 1—21, http://dx.doi.org/10.1037/drm0000099; David Kahn, "Brain basis of self: Self-organization and lessons from dreaming," *Frontiers in Psychology* (2013): https://doi.org/10.3389/fpsyg.2013.00408.

Chapter Two

1. Quote from Zhuangzi in *The Butterfly as Companion: Meditations on the First Three Chapters of the Chuang-Tzu*, Kuang Ming Wu (State University of New York Press, 1990).

2. David Kahn, "Brain basis of self: Self-organization and lessons from dreaming"; Yi-Fu Tuan, *Space and Place: The Perspective of Experience* (University of Minnesota Press, 1977).

3. Tuan, *Space and Place: The Perspective of Experience.*

4. Mabel Elsworth Todd, *The Thinking Body* (Princeton Book Company, 1937).

5. For a discussion of the image-basis of embodied cognition in this reference and throughout this chapter, see, for example: Lawrence W. Barsalou, "Grounded Cognition," *Annual Review of Psychology* 59 (2008): 617—645; Silvan S. Tomkins, *Affect Imagery Consciousness: The Complete Edition* (Springer Publishing Company, 2008); see also the literature on the default network: Buckner, Andrews-Hanna, and Schachter, "The Brain's Default Network: Anatomy, Function, and Relevance to Disease."

6. My gratitude to Anne Baring who first used the image of being in a skinsuit in a talk she gave for the Dream Your World Kids Conference I co-organized in 2017.

7. Barsalou, "Grounded Cognition"; Raymond W. Gibbs, Jr., *Embodiment and Cognitive Science* (Cambridge University Press,

2005); George Lakoff and Mark Johnson, *Metaphors We Live By* (University of Chicago Press, 1981).

8. Lakoff and Johnson, *Metaphors We Live By.*

9. Antonio Damasio, *The Feeling of What Happens: Body and Emotion in the Making of Consciousness* (Harcourt, 1999).

10. This phrase was mentioned by Jane Goodall in a *60 Minutes* episode featuring photographer Thomas Mangelsen, first aired in 2018, and accessed January 26, 2025, at https://www.youtube.com/watch?v=7K8yPhaAZAg&t=1554.

11. David Kahn, "Dream basis of self: Self-organization and lessons from dreaming."

12. Barsalou, "Grounded Cognition"; Eleanor Rosch, Carolyn B. Mervis, Wayne D. Gray, David M. Johnson, and Penny Boyes-Braem, "Basic objects in natural categories," in *Cognitive Psychology: Key Readings*, eds. Balota and Marsh (Psychology Press, 2004), 448—471.

13. Kenneth E. Boulding, *The Image: Knowledge in Life and Society* (University of Michigan Press, 1956); Tomkins, *Affect Imagery Consciousness: The Complete Edition.*

14. See, for example, Andrews-Hanna, "The Brain's Default Network and its Adaptive Role in Internal Mentation"; Gerald Epstein, *Waking Dream Therapy: Unlocking the Secrets of Self Through Dreams and Imagination* (ACMI Press, 1992); Russell Epstein, "Consciousness, art, and the brain: Lessons from Marcel Proust," *Conscious Cognition* 13, no. 2 (2004): 213—240; William James, *The Principles of Psychology* (Henry Holt and Company, 1890).

15. Epstein, *Waking Dream Therapy: Unlocking the Secrets of Self Through Dreams and Imagination.*

16. George Lakoff, "How metaphor structures dreams: The theory of conceptual metaphor applied to dream analysis," in *Dreams: A Reader on Religious, Cultural, and Psychological Dimensions of Dreaming*, ed.

Kelly Bulkeley (Palgrave Macmillan, 2001); Bulkeley speaks to the limitations of this approach in *Big Dreams: The Science of Dreaming and the Origins of Religion.*

17. The human physical experience is explored in the field of perceptual geography. See, for example: Tuan, *Space and Place: The Perspective of Experience.*

Chapter Three

1. The kinds of dreams, and their categories, I learned from Dr. Catherine Shainberg, who taught me this tradition of dreaming.

Chapter Four

1. Narrative structure has been recognized as far back as Aristotle, see also: Neil Cohn, Ray Jackendoff, Phillip J. Holcomb, and Grina R. Kuperberg, "The grammar of visual narrative: Neural evidence for constituent structure in sequential image comprehension," *Neuropsychologia* 64 (2014): 63—70; Carin Whitney, Walter Huber, Juliane Klann, Susanne Weis, Sören Krach, Tilo Kircher, "Neural correlates of narrative shifts during auditory story comprehension," *Neuroimage* 47, no. 1 (2009): 360—366, https://doi.org/10.1016/j.neuroimage.2009.04.037.

2. For a demonstration of minor key incompletion see: Benjamin Zander, "The transformative power of classical music," *TED* YouTube, accessed August 2021, at https://www.youtube.com/watch?v=r9LCwI5iErE.

3. Jan Rummel and Laura Nied, "Do drives drive the train of thought? Effects of hunger and sexual arousal on mind-wandering behavior," *Consciousness and Cognition* 55 (2017): 179—187.

4. Kahn, "Dream basis of self: Self-organization and lessons from dreaming."

Chapter Five

1. Gerald Epstein, *Waking Dream Therapy: Unlocking the Secrets of Self Through Dreams and Imagination.*

2. The four levels, used here with dreams, come from a traditional Talmudic means of textual exegesis in Jewish biblical hermeneutics. Dr. Catherine Shainberg applies this method of inquiry to working with dreams.

Chapter Six

1. Lakoff and Johnson, *Metaphors We Live By*; Tuan, *Space and Place: The Perspective of Experience.*

2. My thanks to Dr. Patrice Saphy, my kinesiotherapist, for this phrase.

3. Roy F. Baumeister, Ellen Bratslavsky, Catrin Finkenauer, and Kathleen D. Vohs, "Bad is Stronger than Good," *Review of General Psychology* 5, no. 4 (2001): 323—370, https://doi.org/10.1037//1089-2680.5.4.323.

4. *Jerusalem Talmud*, Tractate Berachot 55.

Chapter Eight

1. See, for example, William James, who posited the origin of emotion and feeling as physiological. He also treats what he calls the "subtler emotions," such as beauty (which in this chapter we would call Feeling), as originating in the body as a somatic response to a stimulus. James asserts that physiological changes are perceived, and then sensed and named as emotion; e.g. we feel sorry because we cry, versus we cry because we feel sorry; William James, "Chapter XXV: The Emotions," in *The Principles of Psychology* (Henry Holt and Company, 1890); His views have been recently

revisited in the field of neurobiology; see Bruce H. Friedman, "Feelings and the body: The Jamesian perspective on autonomic specificity of emotion," *Biological Psychology* 84 (1994): 383—393; P. J. Lang, "The varieties of emotional experience: A meditation on James-Lange Theory," *Psychological Review* 101, no. 2 (1994): 211—221; see also Damasio, who similarly defines emotion as a physiological response, that includes a mental image, in reaction to a stimulus. Valence given to this set of responses—including the image—determines behavior, underlining the essential role of emotion in decision-making; Antonio R. Damasio, Thomas J. Grabowski, Antoine Bechara, Hanna Damasio, Laura L. B. Ponto, Josef Parvizi, J, and Richard D. Hichwa, "Subcortical and cortical brain activity during the feeling of self-generated emotions," *Nature Neuroscience* 3, no. 10 (2000); Antoine Bechara and Antonio R. Damasio, "The somatic marker hypothesis: A neural theory of economic decision," *Games and Economic Behavior* 52 (2005): 336—372; Antonio R. Damasio and Gil B. Carvalho, "The nature of feelings: Evolutionary and neurobiological origins," *Nature Reviews Neuroscience* 14, no. 2 (2013): 143—52, https://doi.org/10.1038/nrn3403; Antonio R. Damasio and Hanna Damasio, "Exploring the concept of homeostasis and considering its implications for economics," *Journal of Economic Behavior & Organization* 126 (2016): 125—129.

2. The Life Plan was created by Muriel Lasry-Lancri. A version of it and the exercises in this chapter can be found in Catherine Shainberg, *Kabbalah and the Power of Dreaming* (Inner Traditions, 2005). See also, from this same lineage of teachings, Gerald Epstein, *Emotional Mastery*, audio program for American Institute for Mental Imagery; and Phyllis Kahaney and Rachel Epstein, *Reversing the Trauma of War: PTSD Help for Veterans, Active-Duty Personnel and Their Families* (ACMI Press, 2020).

3. Lillian Bridges, *Face Reading in Chinese Medicine* (Churchill Livingstone, 2012).

4. Kajsa Brimdyr, Karin Cadwell, Kristin Svensson, Yuki Takahashi, Eva Nissen, and Ann-Marie Widstrom, "The nine stages of skin-to-skin: Practical guidelines and insights from four countries," *Maternal & Child Nutrition* 16, no. 4 (2020): https://doi.org/10.1111/mcn.13042; Ann-Marie Widstrom, Kajsa Brimdyr, Kristin Svensson, Karin Cadwell, and Eva Nissen, "Skin-to-skin contact the first hour after birth, underlying implications and clinical practice," *Acta Paediatrica* 108 (2019): 1192—1204. These two studies list nine initial stages of newborn behavior, though several of these stages duplicate each other (e.g. relaxing, resting, sleeping). These two studies, focused in large part on breastfeeding, do not list comfort as one of the baby's first stages, though it is implied in several stage descriptions.

5. It is interesting that in traditional Chinese medicine a fundamental tenet is that there is no one expression of a disease—two people may be infected with the same virus, but they won't have the same disease because of the uniqueness of each body and its composition and expression of elements and energy. The bodily imbalance is treated, not the infecting agent. See Bridges, *Face Reading in Chinese Medicine*.

6. James (and Lange, whom he references) describes the deleterious effects on the body correlated to specific emotions; emotions being a block to the balanced flow of fluids in tissues and other homeostatic, physiological functions. See James, *The Principles of Psychology*. Traditional Chinese medicine sees also emotions manifesting in specific physiological ways. In Traditional Chinese medicine face reading, chronically blocked flow shows in the face as hard, white areas corresponding to the organ-energy that is blocked. A giving, pink flush is a normal flowing energy. See Bridges, *Face Reading in Chinese Medicine*.

7. An interesting case study of an executive who noticed he smoked only when irritated: Tony Schwartz and Catherine McCarthy, "Manage Your Energy, Not Your Time," *Harvard Business Review*, October 2007, https://hbr.org/2007/10/manage-your-energy-not-your-time. The

executive broke this pattern by consciously taking breaths instead of reaching for a cigarette. This a perfect example of working the Life Plan. See also C. G. Greeno and R. R. Wing, "Stress-induced eating," *Psychological Bulletin* Volume 115, no. 3 (1994): 444—464; Michael Macht, "How emotions affect eating: A five-way model," *Appetite* 50 (2008): 1—11.

8. Mary Helen Immordino-Yang, Andrea McColl, Hanna Damasio, and Antonio Damasio, "Neural correlates of admiration and compassion," *PNAS (Proceedings of the National Academy of Sciences of the United States of America)* 106, no. 19 (2009): 8021—8026; Glenn R. Fox, Jonas Kaplan, Hanna Damasio, and Antonio Damasio, "Neural correlates of gratitude," *Frontiers in Psychology* 6, Article 1491 (2015): https://doi.org/10.3389/fpsyg.2015.01491.

9. Laura D. Crocker, Wendy Heller, Stacie L. Warren, Amanda J. O'Hare, Zachary P. Infantolino, and Gregory A. Miller, "Relationships among cognition, emotion, and motivation: implications for intervention and neuroplasticity in psychopathology," *Frontiers in Human Neuroscience* 7 (2013); Daniel J. Siegel, *The Developing Mind: How Relationships and the Brain Interact to Shape Who We Are* (Guilford Press, 1999); Daniel J. Siegel, *Mind: A Journey to the Heart of Being Human* (Norton & Company, 2017).

10. Damasio and Damasio, "Exploring the concept of homeostasis and considering its implications for economics."

11. Crocker, Heller, Warren, O'Hare, Infantolino, and Miller, "Relationships among cognition, emotion, and motivation: implications for intervention and neuroplasticity in psychopathology"; Damasio and Damasio, "Exploring the concept of homeostasis and considering its implications for economics"; M. Macht, "Effects of high- and low-energy meals on hunger, physiological processes, and reactions to emotional stress, *Appetite* 26 (1996): 71—88; Rummel and Nied, "Do drives drive the train of thought? Effects of hunger and sexual arousal on mind-wandering behavior."

12. Damasio and Damasio, "Exploring the concept of homeostasis and considering its implications for economics."

Chapter Nine

1. James, *The Principles of Psychology.*

2. Rachel Epstein, "The neural-cognitive basis of the Jamesian stream of thought," *Conciousness and Cognition* 9 (2000): 550—575, https://doi.org/10.1006/ccog.2000.0486.

3. "What is Quantum Physics?" *Caltech Science Exchange*, accessed on January 28, 2024, at https://scienceexchange.caltech.edu/topics/quantum-science-explained/quantum-physics.

4. Rupert Sheldrake, "Is the Sun Conscious?" *Journal of Consciousness Studies* 28, no. 2-4 (2021): 8—28.

5. R' Bana'ah, in the Jewish Gemara, Beresheit Folio 55b.

Chapter Ten

1. Colette, the teacher of this dreamwork referenced in the Introduction, used to say that one of her greatest gifts was knowing how to catch the moment.

Chapter Eleven

1. Abdulla and Cramond, "After Six Decades of Systematic Study of Creativity: What Do Teachers Need to Know About What It Is and How It Is Measured?"; Bronson and Merryman, "The Creativity Crisis."; Shellenbarger, "A Box? Or a Spaceship? What Makes Kids Creative?"

2. Kim, "The Creativity Crisis: The Decrease in Creative Thinking Scores on the Torrance Tests of Creative Thinking."

3. Bronson and Merryman, "The Creativity Crisis."

4. Andrews, "Creative skills and digital literacy: Equipping the next generation for success."

5. "The Bloomberg Recruiter Report: Job Skills Companies Want But Can't Get," *Bloomberg* (blog).

6. Described in Bronson and Merryman, "The Creativity Crisis."

7. Richards, *Everyday Creativity and New Views of Human Nature: Psychological, Social, and Spiritual Perspectives.*

8. Ibid.

9. S. Acar and M. A. Runco, "Assessing associative distance among ideas elicited by tests of divergent thinking," *Creativity Research Journal* 26, no. 2 (2014): 229—238, https://www.doi.org/10.1080/10400419.2014.901095; Sureyya Yoruk and Mark A. Runco, "The Neuroscience of Divergent Thinking," *ANS: Journal for Neurocognitive Research, Activitas Nervosa Superior* 56, no. 1-2 (2014).

10. Kahn, "Brain basis of self: Self-organization and lessons from dreaming."

11. Acar and Runco, "Assessing associative distance among ideas elicited by tests of divergent thinking"; Yoruk and Runco, "The Neuroscience of Divergent Thinking."

12. Mark A. Runco, "Simplifying theories of creativity and revisiting the criterion problem: A comment on Simonton's (2009) hierarchical model of domain-specific disposition, development, and achievement," *Perspectives on Psychological Science* 4, no. 5.

13. Buckner, Andrews-Hanna, and Schacter, "The brain's default network: Anatomy, function, and relevance to disease."

14. McNamara, *The Neuroscience of Sleep and Dreams.*

15. Kahn, "Brain basis of self: self-organization and lessons from dreaming."

16. Ibid.

17. Runco, "Simplifying theories of creativity and revisiting the criterion problem: A comment on Simonton's (2009) hierarchical model of domain-specific disposition, development and achievement."

18. Robert S. Root-Bernstein and Michele M. Root-Bernstein, *Sparks of Genius: The Thirteen Thinking Tools of Creative People* (Houghton, 2000); Runco, "Simplifying theories of creativity and revisiting the criterion problem: A comment on Simonton's (2009) hierarchical model of domain-specific disposition, development and achievement."

19. Abdulla and Cramond, "After Six Decades of Systematic Study of Creativity: What Do Teachers Need to Know About What It Is and How It Is Measured?"; Pamela Burnard, Anna Craft, Teresa Cremin, Bernadette Duffy, Ruth Hanson, Jean Keene, Lindsay Haynes, and Dawn Burns, "Documenting 'possibility thinking': A journey of collaborative enquiry," *International Journal of Early Years Education* 14, no. 3 (2006): 243—262; Ware, *Visual Thinking for Design*.

20. David Jones, *The Aha! Moment: A Scientist's Take on Creativity* (Johns Hopkins University Press, 2012).

21. Roland, "13 World-Changing Ideas that Came from Dreams (Literally)."

22. Sue Robertson, "Imagine Better—Imagine More! Don't be content with the status quo. Turn on your creativity and imagination to fuel innovations in our professions. . . and your career," *The ASHA Leader*, accessed on December 2019, at https://leader.pubs.asha.org 140.234.253.9.

23. Runco, "Simplifying theories of creativity and revisiting the criterion problem: A comment on Simonton's (2009) hierarchical model of domain-specific disposition, development and achievement."

24. Kahn, "Brain basis of self: Self-organization and lessons from dreaming."

25. Jouvet, *The Paradox of Sleep: The Story of Dreaming.*

26. Barsalou, "Grounded Cognition."

27. Richards uses a similar phrase to describe the transformative power of art. Richards, *Everyday Creativity and New Views of Human Nature: Psychological, Social, and Spiritual Perspectives.*

28. Sheldrake, "Is the Sun Conscious?"

29. Hugh Brody, *Maps and Dreams: Indians and the British Columbia Frontier* (J. Norman and Hobhouse, 1982); Kelly Bulkeley, "Dreaming is imaginative play in sleep: A theory of the function of dreams," *American Psychological Association: Dreaming* 29, no. 1 (2019): 1—29; McNamara, *The Neuroscience of Sleep and Dreams.*

30. "7 Great Examples of Scientific Discoveries Made in Dreams," *Famous Scientists: The Art of Genius*, accessed on June 22, 2022, at https://www.famousscientists.org/7-great-examples-of-scientific-discoveries-made-in-dreams/; Roland, "13 World-Changing Ideas that Came from Dreams (Literally)"; Alex Salamanca, "25 Dreams That Forever Changed Society," list25.com, accessed on June 22, 2022, at https://list25.com/25-dreams-that-forever-changed-society/; Larry Page, "University of Michigan Commencement Address, Spring 2009."

Acknowledgments

Like all books, this book has many midwives, and I am grateful for their incredible support. Ina Gjikondi planted the seed to write it and has been a continual support, including during moments in our work together when I needed to pause in order to write. Ina sent me to Beth Grossman who listened to me ramble then put her finger on a sentence and said: "That's what you need to write about." Beth sent me to my incredible agent, Leslie Meredith, who took that sentence and expanded it, and my imagination, making a real manuscript and real project—I am forever grateful. Through Leslie I met Sarah "Superstar" Kelley who taught me how to think and write from the shoes of the reader, both visually and in words, around the book and in our outreach beyond it. To Scott Hatch for coming up with the best title ever! To everyone at Urano World/Urano US, especially my wonderful editor Suzy Swartz for developing the work, including and especially "The.Big.Note." that changed everything, and for her rich creativity in thinking through the visual elements of the book—it is a joy to work with you! To Jamie Wood for precise copy edits and great suggestions for the last chapter, Amanda Weiss for designing such a fantastic cover, Damian Cubells for the interior design, and James Faccinto for the publicity: thank you all! To Katalin Pula at Poppypress for the Life Plan designs and ongoing visual collaboration. To Jennifer Lukomski, Sabine Adam Fischer, and Jennifer Sun who read clunky early drafts and gave great notes, Betta Eichner for thinking about visual elements, Anna Nowicka for ongoing dream discussions, and all my fellow practitioners and students at the Institute who supported me in every step of the marathon, and for every great question that continues to help hone the work—thank you so much for this incredible journey. To Catherine Shainberg for the early years of dream teaching. And to my nephew Will Buckner, who has patiently read sections, examined sentences, brainstormed, encouraged, and inspired me at every step—you are always my favorite dreamer to discuss ideas with.

About the Author

Photo credit: Guillaume Estève

Bonnie Buckner, PhD, is the founder and CEO of the International Institute for Dreaming and Imagery®, where she brings dreamwork to organizations and individuals in such diverse fields as leadership, the performing and creative arts, academia, and in programs aimed at developing youth. She also serves as Co-Faculty Director for The George Washington University's Center for Excellence in Public Leadership's e-Co Leadership Coaching Certification Program, where she uses dreaming and imagery work to help develop coaches.

When Bonnie is not teaching, she is still dreaming in France.

To learn more about dreaming work, join a class, or to bring dream-work to your organization, please visit:

https://institutefordreamingandimagery.com/

or email us at info@institutefordreamingandimagery.com

To follow the Institute:

dreamwithiidi
institutefordreamingandimagery